Praise for

WALK IT OFF

"A **page-turning and inspiring** journey of recovery . . . Hilarious and hopeful."

LISA GENOVA, bestselling author of *Still Alice*

"I can't remember the last time I've liked a character in a book so much—only this one is real. . . . Ruth Marshall's story is **filled with heart and courage and heaping spoonfuls of humor.**"

GLENN DIXON, #1 bestselling author of *Juliet's Answer*

"Funny, heartfelt, and well written . . . **Profound and witty.** I could not put it down."

KARMA BROWN, bestselling author of *Come Away with Me*

"A moving and hilarious portrayal of what happens when our bodies get the best of us and life is turned upside down . . . **Wry and honest and wickedly funny,** *Walk It Off* is a wonderful debut memoir from a **writer to watch.**"

AMY STUART, bestselling author of *Still Mine*

"A **hilarious account** of the kind of thing we all pray doesn't happen to us . . . An epic journey of recovery that is equally scary and funny."

MICHAEL REDHILL, two-time Scotiabank Giller Prize nominee

"Ruth Marshall writes with unblinking honesty and intimate charm about the challenges and triumphs of medical calamity. **The pages practically turn themselves.**"

TEVA HARRISON, award-winning author of *In-Between Days*

"So funny, so **achingly poignant** . . . Ruth's story is **riveting,** her warmth and honesty irresistible."

JAMES CHATTO, author of *The Greek for Love*

"**Revelatory, human, gutting, and funny** . . . Taking a simple step will never feel the same. One of those books you can't put down and you will insist that everyone you love has to read. Ruth is us, at our worst and most brave."

DIANE FLACKS, actor, author of *Bear with Me*

WALK IT OFF

THE TRUE AND HILARIOUS STORY OF HOW I LEARNED TO STAND,
WALK, PEE, RUN, AND HAVE SEX AGAIN AFTER A NIGHTMARISH
DIAGNOSIS TURNED MY AWESOME LIFE UPSIDE DOWN

RUTH MARSHALL

A MEMOIR

PUBLISHED BY SIMON & SCHUSTER
New York   London   Toronto   Sydney   New Delhi

SIMON &
SCHUSTER
CANADA

Simon & Schuster Canada
A Division of Simon & Schuster, Inc.
166 King Street East, Suite 300
Toronto, Ontario M5A 1J3

This Simon & Schuster Canada edition January 2018

SIMON & SCHUSTER CANADA and colophon are registered trademarks of Simon & Schuster, Inc.

For information about special discounts for bulk purchases, please contact Simon & Schuster Special Sales at 1-800-268-3216 or CustomerService@simonandschuster.ca.

Interior design by Carly Loman

Manufactured in the United States of America

10 9 8 7 6 5 4 3 2 1

Library and Archives Canada Cataloguing in Publication

Marshall, Ruth, author
Walk it off : the true and hilarious story of how I learned to stand, walk, pee, run, and have sex again after a nightmarish diagnosis turned my awesome life upside down / Ruth Marshall.
Issued in print and electronic formats.
ISBN 978-1-5011-7362-2 (hardcover).—ISBN 978-1-5011-7368-4 (ebook)
1. Marshall, Ruth—Health. 2. Marshall, Ruth. 3. Meningioma—Patients—Canada—Biography. 4. Brain—Tumors—Patients—Canada—Biography. 5. Meningioma—Popular works. 6. Actresses—Canada—Biography. I. Title.
RC280.M4M37 2018 362.1968'20092 C2017-904177-0
C2017-904178-9

ISBN 978-1-5011-7362-2
ISBN 978-1-5011-7368-4 (ebook)

For Rich
And for our boys, Joey and Henry

CONTENTS

WALK IT OFF

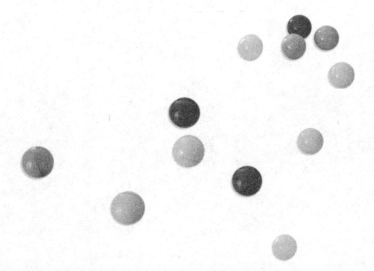

PART ONE

out of step

1

Losing My Footing

MARCH 2012, 4:30 A.M.

I watched as my parents pulled into the driveway right on schedule—fifteen minutes early. I moved down the stairs as quickly as my confused feet would allow, trying to beat my dad to the house before he knocked and woke up Rich and the kids, but I was not quick enough. He rapped on the door as if it were mid-afternoon; a nice confident knuckling. I opened the door.

"I'll just be a sec, Dad. Everyone's asleep. I'll meet you in the car." I closed the door.

My father's smile was too wide, his eyes crinkled unnaturally, his stance was uncertain.

I was in the clothes I had laid out the night before: black sweat pants, black T-shirt, black hoodie, black trench. *Christ*, I thought as I looked in the mirror, *I'm a vampire.* I was even wearing a black bra. Most mornings when I am hooking my bra into place, Rich, my husband of sixteen years, perks up. "Whoa!" he'll say, as if seeing my boobs for the first time instead of the ten thousandth. But on that morning, his response was more sober.

3

"I doubt you'll be able to keep your bra on during the MRI," he said.

I gave him a look. Decorum, plus the size of my breasts, dictates that I wear a bra, in every situation, always.

Rich wanted to take me to the hospital, but I didn't want to leave the boys alone at such an early hour of the morning, even though, at eleven and fourteen, I'm sure they would have been fine. "Besides," I told him, "my parents need something constructive to do with their concern." I knew my mom and dad had been secretly talking to everyone about me, consulting the Internet, matching up every theory they had with what Google had to say, commiserating with their friends, taking stock of their own bodies' failings to see if anything I had lined up with anything they had. It was almost laughable how one innocuous observation had snowballed to this moment.

●

"Why do you keep staring at your shoes?" the soprano beside me had asked just a few weeks earlier.

Every Thursday night, a bunch of middle-aged Jews gathered to sing in the sanctuary of our local synagogue. Somewhere between the beginning of practice and coffee cake break, I became aware of my feet. "They're asleep," I said. "I feel like they've been asleep for a few days now."

"You should see my doctor," she said, without hesitation. "Actually, he's a chiropractor, but he's also magical."

I took down his name.

The next morning, I woke up, but my feet didn't.

"They're still tingling," I said to Rich before the alarm went off. He wasn't technically awake yet. I kicked him a little.

"Mmmm," he said.

"Weird, right?"

"Mmmm."

"But not *that* weird."

"Mmmm."

"Oh, forget it."

"Mm-hmm."

The following week I told my mother about the weird feeling, and the week after that I interrupted the arm-buffing part of my personal training session to tell my trainer.

"You should have an MRI," she said, reacting swiftly to my tone, which caused me to react swiftly to hers.

"Do you think it's MS?"

My trainer sat back on her heels and studied me. "I think your feet shouldn't be tingling."

I saw my GP, Dr. Bright, the next day. Remembering her weakness for pretty shoes, I was quick to comment on the new cherry-red ones she was wearing. She looked both flush and fresh, as if maybe she had just had sex with her boyfriend in the patient file room moments before our appointment. I had never noticed all the posters on her office wall. I commented on each one. I asked about her daughter, and her daughter's boyfriend, and her daughter's job prospects, and her daughter's boyfriend's job prospects, and if she thought the weather felt uncharacteristically dry for spring.

Eventually, Dr. Bright cut in. "What's up, Ruth? I usually see you only for strep throat."

"Oh, it's nothing. It's nothing. It's stupid actually."

"Okay . . ." Dr. Bright said, waiting.

"Well, my feet have been feeling tingly and numb for the past, oh, few weeks now, and I looked up some stuff on the Internet and I know I'm too old to have MS—nice to be too old in some cases I guess—haha! So I know that's not the problem but it does seem a little weird so I thought maybe you could poke me or something and also, just a side thought, I wondered if maybe I should have an MRI to rule out the possibility of MS—not that anyone even *suggested* that to me but anyway is your hair different?"

Dr. Bright didn't answer. "Is one leg giving you trouble or both?"

"It's not my legs," I said. "It's my feet."

"So your legs aren't bothering you?"

"Well, the strangeness does seem to have moved up my legs somewhat. *Somewhat.*"

She asked again if one leg was more problematic than the other. It felt like a trick question where neither answer was incorrect but one answer was *more* correct than the other. In the end, to stop her questions and to stop myself from saying anything more, I decided to cry. Dr. Bright stood over me for a moment with her arms crossed, observing me. I am not a crier. She went to her computer and started tapping. A piece of paper shot out of the printer. She passed it to me, still warm.

"What's this?"

"A requisition for an MRI. I'll book the appointment right away."

I looked at Dr. Bright. Her face was redder than when I'd arrived. "Do you think I have MS?"

"I really don't know, Ruth, but we should probably find out. And here's a referral for a neurologist."

She ripped a piece of paper from her prescription pad.

"And I'm red because I'm having a hot flash," she said, putting the backs of her hands against her cheeks. "Try to relax," she said as I got up to go. But I wasn't sure if she was talking to herself or to me.

•

My MRI was booked quickly, only two weeks out from my appointment with Dr. Bright. To offset increasing worry in the days leading up to it, I decided to change my perspective. Maybe having tingly feet wasn't so bad. *It's kind of cute*, I told myself. *No one ever died from the tingles, right?*

I asked around.

"It's because you wear high heels too much," Karen, my older sister, said.

"It's the hot yoga," said my mom. "I don't trust it."

"How the heck am I supposed to know?" said Joey, my fourteen-year-old son.

And then there was Rich. "It might just be age, hon." While this theory made the most sense, it was also the most depressing. We were walking in the ravine near our home, part of our Sunday-morning routine. "You can't get around the fact that your body is changing."

"I thought I was getting around that fact just fine," I said.

We linked arms and looked at my feet as we walked; they appeared to be doing their job perfectly well. So what if some extra tingling came with age? Tingling, after all, did come with some rather pleasing effects.

But that was then. Now here I was with my parents, on the way to Toronto Western Hospital, my MRI requisition tucked inside my purse, at four thirty in the morning, an hour when nothing good ever happens. It was so early the front doors of the hospital were locked. My parents and I had to walk through the alley to a side entrance, a dark wind pulling our hair up and swirling our coats around our legs. An enthusiastic security guard rushed to meet us at the door.

"Sorry, sorry," he said, as if he were late. He held the door for us, the wind straining his arm.

In the reception area, I filled out a form.

Do you have an eyelid spring? No.

Do you have any shrapnel in your body? No.

Did you tell your husband that your feet aren't the only limbs that are tingling?

I blinked several times until the question disappeared.

There were other patients waiting, some also filling in forms. The MRI department was a twenty-four-hour, seven-day-a-week business, and as far as I could tell, business was booming. My parents quietly read their books: two fake pictures of calm. I left to change into a hospital gown. I was allowed to keep my underwear, shoes, and socks on, but Rich was right—the bra came off; the machine didn't like metal or wires. I had taken an Ativan as soon as I woke up that morning so I could stay still during the MRI. Outside the curtained stall, I sat on the green plastic chair wearing two hospital gowns—one covering my boobs, the other covering my bum. The mottled black-and-white floor caught my attention and I tried, using only the power of my mind, to make all the tiny black dots converge into one giant black dot. That's how the male nurse found me, elbows on my knees, face in my palms, captivated by the floor.

"We're ready for you, Ms. Marshall."

I lay down on the table and discreetly readjusted my gowns. The Ativan had melted inside me, thick and sweet, flowing straight down to my toes. They felt coated with good news. I smiled at the male nurse and the male nurse smiled back at me. He handed me a rubbery button to press in case I felt panicky, then he slid me inside the tubular MRI machine. I was content, at peace, high. This was going to be so easy.

My thoughts swayed gently, silky tendrils in the sea, sweeping lazily back and forth, reaching lower and lower. As they neared bottom, my thoughts found a little snag. The tendrils caught it, picked at it, combed it back up to me for examination. It wobbled close; I could just make out its lineaments. Yes, there was definitely something there. I tried to blink the image away, but it kept bobbing in front of me. It was bigger than an amoeba, bigger than an avocado. I gripped the rubbery panic button.

It was the size of a grenade.

•

In a matter of days, Dr. Shure, the neurologist I'd been referred to, had my MRI results. She mulled aloud over terms she'd learned in medical school but had rarely encountered since.

"Blake's pouch cyst, arachnoid cyst, ventricular enlargement . . . Ah! Hydrocephalus!" she exclaimed.

I shrugged.

"You know those really big-headed kids?"

"Yep."

"Their heads are like that because they have water on the brain. And so do you, although it doesn't seem to have ever bothered you. In fact, none of these conditions seemed to have bothered you."

Actually, I was thinking, *you're kind of bothering me.*

She tested the strength in my legs and arms. She placed a tuning fork against my feet, clanged it, and asked me to tell her when I felt the buzzing stop. She pressed the palm of her hand against my forehead and asked me to push against it as hard as I could. She brushed her hand up my left leg, the leg that had become more numb and tingly in recent days.

"How does that feel?" she asked.

"Fine."

"Normal?"

"Sure." I hesitated. "How *should* it feel?"

"Sometimes people with nerve issues will say that it feels as if they're being touched through cloth."

"Oh."

That was exactly how it felt but I remained stubbornly silent. I also didn't tell her about my thighs.

"Does that feel hot to you?" I had asked Rich only days before, pressing his hand against my inner thigh where the sensation was most pronounced.

"I always think you're hot," he said. I looked at him and waited. "No, it doesn't feel hot."

Hours later, pressing his hand on the same spot. "Freezing cold, right?"

"Sorry, babe—not to me. It just feels like a thigh."

"You have huge calves!" Dr. Shure said, startling me. "I mean they are really huge. But the rest of you is so small. And your arms are so skinny!"

"I know." I have been told both these things my whole life.

"You wait here. I'm just going to slip out and take some notes."

She came back a while later with a marked uptick of excitement, one that drew her to her full height. "I've got it! Neuromuscular disease!" It was as if she had been searching her office, turned the place upside down, and then found the two words attached to each other like Lego pieces under a sheaf of papers.

"No, no, no," I said, wagging my finger. "I don't have a disease."

"Then let's call it a muscle *disorder*," she said, practically rolling her eyes. "But I have to tell you." She leaned in very close, letting me in on a secret. "I've seen only three cases like this in all my years as a neurologist." She was smiling, astounded, I think, by her good luck. "And you're the third!"

"You mean, people with big calves and skinny arms?"

"Precisely!"

She wrote down the name and number of a neuromuscular neurologist and told me to make an appointment with him straight away. "I can't just ignore this," she said.

But I could, and I did. I left her office with the name of this new neurologist already lost in the detritus at the bottom of my purse.

I come from a long line of short people with skinny arms and big calves. Common sense told me this was not an extraordinary condition.

I went home and told Rich and then I called my parents.

"It appears that I'm fine, but the neurologist is nuts," I said. We had a good laugh over her skinny arms/meaty calves obsession, and then spent some time enumerating those members of our family in possession of both.

Meanwhile, in the days that followed, I became increasingly clumsy and tentative. Stairs gave me pause, as did curbs and sidewalk cracks. My feet acted like they were drunk trying to act like they were sober.

I met my friend Michael for breakfast. Before we ordered, I made him watch me walk across the restaurant. I wanted to know if he thought my gait seemed different. He claimed not to notice any change. I didn't feel relieved, only more anxious. Was it possible that this whole tingly mess was in my head? I worried about pursuing this train of thought with my friend. Although he is a deep thinker with clever insights and a uniquely unmasculine ability to discuss a thing to death, he is also on constant alert for potential health catastrophes—his own as well as others. (Before his first sip of coffee that morning, he told me that his eye twitching clearly pointed to ALS.)

"Are you worried?" he asked me, already worried himself. "About your feet?"

"Not really."

"Really?"

"Really."

Believing me, he double-checked that his swallow reflex was still in good working order, then swiped the last of my bagel.

•

"It's me," Rich said.

"It's not you, babe."

"But it *must* be me."

"I'm telling you, it isn't. It's *me*. Something's wrong with *me*."

What Dr. Shure had said, about patients with nerve issues feeling as though they were being touched through cloth, that was happening to me—but the area of impairment stretched higher than I had been willing to admit. Yes, my feet and legs felt covered in cloth. But there was also the matter of my *hoochie*. It felt covered in cloth, too—all the time—even naked, *especially* naked. My sex life with Rich was going off the rails. I considered faking it, just to tide us over until things sprang back to normal, but I couldn't go through with it. I had only ever pulled that stunt once—not with Rich, but some other guy, a hundred years ago. Now, feeling desperate, I called my girlfriend Joanie to offload my worry, believing that since she lived in a different country, the friendship rule of marital-sex-nondisclosure didn't apply. As soon as she realized where my story was headed, she began yelling frantically into her cell. "*Hannah! Hannah! Hannah!*" Her ten-year-old daughter was in the car and I was on speakerphone.

As happy as I was to speculate on the frequency and hotness of other people's sex lives (the butchers at Nortown, our next-door neighbors, every Real Housewife), I never discussed my own. Mum has always been the word. Mum, not numb.

I made another appointment with my GP, Dr. Bright.

"I seem to be a little frozen." I pointed. "Down there."

"What about your feet and legs?" she asked.

"Same."

Dr. Bright tapped away on her computer.

"I didn't tell the neurologist about *this*," I admitted, pointing again *down there*, like a three-year-old incapable of using her words.

"I can see that," she said, looking over Dr. Shure's report.

"Just tell me you've had other patients with this same numb clitoris thing." I tripped over the word. I have never known where to put the emphasis: *clit*oris or clit*oris*.

She stopped tapping and swiveled in her chair to face me.

"Ruth, you're an enigma."

It struck me that this is the kind of thing you want to hear only from a lover when you're naked in bed and you've just said something really off topic but still terrifically sexy.

"Just give me a pill," I said. "Seriously, any pill. Just make it go away."

"I wish I could. But I don't know what to make of this," she said.

My file was open and she was using her lap as a table. I didn't like the urgency with which she was taking notes. I didn't like how quickly she passed me a copy of my file, or the intensity with which she urged me to make another appointment with the neurologist. I could feel my internal circuitry shorting out from worry, my mind pinging and popping with electric anxiety.

"Maybe you should try reading a sexy book. Watch some porn. Might get things moving down there."

"Ha!" I said, a little too loudly. It seemed absurd to be obsessing over my sex life when my feet, legs, hoochie, and increasingly, my bum were slowly disappearing. *What will my life be like if I cannot properly feel what the hell is going on when I'm having sex? What will that mean for my happiness?* Maybe I was just being greedy. We'd had a good run of it, Rich and I. Shouldn't the memory of sixteen years of good sex tide me over for the rest of my life? I played a game called *What would I rather live without: the ability to walk or the ability to have an orgasm?* My answer changed every time I played, which was every other minute.

I read the notes in the file Dr. Bright had given me. *"Perineal numbness . . . This is a patient who never complains . . . Please explore."* I took the file home with me, but I didn't make another appointment with the neurologist. I didn't have time to dwell on my multiple concerns and what they might mean. I had a busy life to live, the needs of my children to be met, and a trip to pack for: The next day, our whole family was leaving for Peru.

•

In the days leading up to our July departure, Rich and I were locked in a game of chicken. Each time he sat at the computer to nail down the details of our trip, he would turn to me and say, "Babe, are you sure we should do this? I can easily cancel the whole thing."

It was true—he could have canceled the whole thing, but that it could be done easily was a lie. There would be penalties to pay, trip guides to terminate, flight money lost, and, most worrisome, the need to face the fact that although I wasn't sick, I definitely wasn't well.

I had tried to be vigilant about getting to the bottom of things. I had kept all my doctor's appointments, met with the magical chiropractor, had an MRI, stopped wearing high heels, cut out my hot yoga practice. I was doing everything right, but still, I was afraid to go. I had some serious trust issues with my body but was zealous in overcompensating so my kids would never know. I challenged them to Ping-Pong tournaments just so I could prove to myself how coordinated I was, when all I wanted to do was lie down and keep a wary eye on my feet. Or I encouraged them to go on bike rides with me even though I was half convinced my numb bum would veer off the seat if my tingling feet didn't get trapped under the pedals first. I would sometimes swallow my aggravation at how much they were enjoying their lives, while also patting myself on the back for hiding my fears from them so brilliantly.

For years before this, Rich and I had discussed taking the kids on an adventure holiday. Now, when we were finally on the cusp of committing to this trip, I felt the least capable of doing it. How could I possibly hike the Inca Trail when I could barely make it from the driveway to our house without tripping?

In the smallest hours of the night when both of us pretended to be asleep, a fearful presence rested between us, the size and weight of a sick child. We took care not to jostle it, not to awaken it; if we just let it rest, maybe everything would be okay.

The trip moved forward.

•

"Lima is a donkey's belly."

I didn't know what our Peruvian guide had meant when she said this—until the last day of our trip. We had to stay in Lima overnight. The sand on the beach was gray, the water was gray, the sky was gray. Even though it was chilly, the air felt heavy. We ducked into our jackets as if the clouds were pressing down on us. I moved through that day like a ghost, biding my time, masking my worry, checking my watch, just wanting to board the damn plane already and be gone. At the airport, we passed a tiny nail salon.

"I've got an idea," Rich said. "Why don't you treat yourself to a foot massage?" He didn't know that over the past five months pedicures had not gone well for me. I half sobbed when my feet were touched. The foam space-keepers that separated my toes after a polish were padded instruments of torture. Rubbing a pumice stone on my heels made me hyperventilate. But I continued to submit myself to these monthly appointments because to do otherwise would indicate a problem, and I had already decided that there wasn't one.

"That's a great idea, babe," I said, smiling.

I grabbed hold of the plush armrests, twisting in my seat and grimacing while my feet were massaged with exfoliating cream—a cream that seemed to have been concocted from glass shards, barbed wire, and cactus. Rich came by to check on me.

"All good?"

"All great!" I was smiling so hard he took a picture of me with his phone. Once the torture was over, I slipped my flats back on and walked unsteadily to our gate. What if someone tried to kidnap the children? What if we were being chased? What if a fire suddenly engulfed the terminal—would I be able to run?

"I'm sorry," I said to the two airport staff as they attempted to shuffle us more quickly to our gate, as we were, literally, running behind. "I can only go this fast."

They seemed to gather that there was some unexplained issue and slowed down. We made our flight on time and headed first to Miami. As soon as we landed, I called my sister.

"Please get me an appointment with the neurologist, Dr. Shure."

"Are you okay?"

"And an appointment with Dr. Bright."

"Oh no. Are you—"

"The earliest appointment possible."

•

The second our cab pulled up to the house, I regretted my dramatic call to my sister at the airport. There was absolutely no reason not to think that all that climbing in Peru had taken a toll on my body. Plus, there was the altitude. The truth was, I was a woman in my late forties who kept asking her body to act like it was thirty.

"I'm canceling my appointments," I told Rich that night, after we had gotten our exhausted boys to bed.

"Why would you do that?"

"Because this is dumb. I've had an MRI, which said explicitly that nothing was wrong with me. We just climbed a mountain for *seven hours* and my body just needs a break. Doesn't yours?"

He said nothing.

"Anyway, the kids are leaving for camp in a few days and I will have the entire month to put my feet up and rest. I'll be fine. I *am* fine."

"Ru, I think you should keep your appointments."

But my decision was made.

I called my friend Paula, who wanted to hear all about our trip, but it was the last thing I wanted to talk about.

"How are your feet?" she asked.

"Oh, you know. Tingly still, but all right."

"Ruthie, can I say something without you getting mad?"

"I'm already mad."

"Maybe you should consider having another MRI."

"No point. There's nothing wrong."

"But maybe you should get one more?"

"Sex is weird."

"What? Oh, that's—oh."

"I can't feel things the same way."

There was a long, awful silence. Paula has always known the right thing to say to me, but not this time. As soon as we hung up, I called the neurologist.

"I'd like to rebook my appointment," I said. "And I need another MRI."

"This is ridiculous!" my mother barked into the phone.

"No, it's not, Mom," I barked back. "The neurologist said this is not an emergency. She can't just snap her fingers and get me another MRI right away."

"It's been five months since the last one and nothing has changed. You're getting worse, not better. We're going to Buffalo."

"*That's* ridiculous."

"We're going. Hang up the phone and make the appointment right now!"

It didn't matter that I was a grown woman; I still did what my mother told me. Three phone calls and two days later, we were on our way to Buffalo.

Cheery John, the MRI technician, set me up inside the capsule. He was short and moved like a garden gnome come to life. His smile said: *This is all routine—we'll have you out of here with a clean bill of health lickety split!* I was grateful for his cheer. I had no choice but to do my MRI drug-free this time—I was the designated driver. While I did manage to doze for the first few minutes, remaining still soon became impossible. The back of my head was throbbing in one spot as if a nail were being pushed slowly, relentlessly, inexorably into it. I hummed along with my breath. I pictured my belly moving up and down. I tried to remember the lyrics to all the songs I knew. I counted backward from a hundred until the numbers collapsed into one another. My heart jumped wildly like it was leaping from one hot coal to the next. I pressed the rubbery panic button and the clanging inside the capsule immediately stopped. Cheery John rushed in and eased me out of the machine.

"What is it, Ruth? Are you all right?"

"I need to know how much longer this is going to be."

I still wasn't allowed to move. I hoped he could hear me. Between the earplugs and the little foam pillows around my head, I wasn't sure if I had spoken out loud.

"The doctor on the other end tells me the pictures he's getting are real good! But the thing is, Ruth, he wants me to inject a dye into your arm so we can get a real clear look in a couple areas. It's called a contrast dye and it's—"

"How long?"

"I'll have to program the machine to get a better idea."

"Fine."

"You know these things don't happen for free, right, Ruth?"

"It's okay. Just do it."

"Alrighty, then, Ruth. Let's just get that dye in ya, okay?"

He lifted my arm to put the needle in and I turned my head just a little so the tears could run sideways.

It was one minute then one minute then three minutes then four minutes and I went through the Beatles songbook that sits on the piano where my younger son, Henry, and I practiced "Let It Be" as a duet for his piano recital just two months earlier. I couldn't remember the words and I couldn't remember the chords and the pounding of the machine as the slides took pictures of my spine matched the imaginary nail going into my head, which matched the words written on the computer chip inside my ears that was trying to brainwash me. Both my hands were sweating and the tingling in my legs had turned ice cold. I couldn't feel my legs or my feet or my torso and I thought I was paralyzed. I jerked my legs to wake them and then panicked that I had screwed up the pictures by moving and would have to start the whole process from the beginning. Cheery John said, "Just ten minutes more," and I started to count to sixty over and over, but I couldn't count past thirty-eight and I couldn't remember the words to "O Canada" and then almost two hours later it was over.

I took my time sitting up. Cheery John was there, holding his arm out toward me. I wiped my damp eyes and then bunched the front of the green hospital gown in my hands.

"Did you tell my mom I was going to be a little longer?" I whispered.

"Oh, yes, Ruth. Don't worry. She knows. She's waitin' for ya."

"Thank you, John."

I picked up my purse and clutched it like a shield. I walked back to the cubicle to change. I sat down on the little stool to pull on my jeans and let out one last terror-stricken moan before I shoved my companions—Worry and Fear—into a private closet inside my brain and kicked the door shut. Already, I had forgotten what it was like to move through the world largely unburdened. As I walked toward my mother, I tried to laugh. "Sorry that took so long, Mom!" My big smile was almost outmatched by her big smile.

"No problem! They told me you'd be a little longer. They're very nice here."

"Very nice," I said.

"Very nice," she said.

"Very," I said.

"Nice," she said.

We got back in the car and drove home. We did not mention the MRI ever again.

•

The sky was unusually dark for an August evening. We arrived at my house and I waved to my mother as she got in her own car to go home to my father and talk about me. I walked into my house without turning on any lights, dropped my bag at the door, and headed upstairs. Rich wasn't home from work yet; the kids were still at overnight camp—I was completely alone. I tore my jeans off before I reached my room. They were driving my legs mad, had been all day, but I thought that wearing them instead of leggings—the only clothing I was comfortable in anymore—would mean that I was still normal, and normal people are able to wear pants without wanting to rip their hair out. My thighs and calves looked like they had always looked but felt ravaged by a thousand tiny cuts. I leaned on my dresser and clasped my hands under my chin. I closed my eyes.

"Listen, I don't really know how to begin this conversation since I only call on you when I fly, but tonight I need your assistance in just one small matter and I'm not going to promise that I'll never ask anything of you again if you help me, because I have children and a husband who I love more than myself, but something is very wrong with me. I know Cheery John saw something bad on my MRI, so all I'm asking is this: Please God, don't let it be cancer."

•

I wanted to be an actress from the time I was six years old and have been one since I was twenty-five. My career has been notable for three reasons: I got naked in my first film role; I was in a television series with Billy Ray Cyrus; and for eight seasons I played a mom on the Canadian teen drama *Degrassi*. The biggest chunk of my career, however, has been made up of commercial voice work. My voice has sold everything from Ikea kitchens to condoms.

The day after I went to Buffalo, I had a voice-over gig for Shoppers Drug Mart, a frequent client. It was hot as hell out and the air-conditioning in my house was wheezy at best. I was already having second thoughts about blow-drying my hair, knowing that

I would only start sweating again the second I was done. I kept up a gentle, mantra-like monologue in my head to help me slow down and redirect my focus away from the looming results of my MRI and onto the little things, like: Was it a stupid idea to wear silk on a sweltering August day? I decided that the uplifting periwinkle blue of the dress canceled out practicalities. I shaved my legs. I wore gold-and-silver sandals that tied up around my ankles. I wore a long silver necklace with a green teardrop pendant. I put on mascara. I looked at myself in my full-length mirror. My tingly feet fought the urge to escape my sandals. They were unwilling to accept anything but total nakedness while I was unwilling to accept such brattiness; pants were optional, shoes were not.

I was able to stand for the entire voice session, ignoring the temptation to rest on the stool behind me. Neither the producers nor my voice partner seemed to notice the effort it took for me to remain perfectly upright, making me wonder for the thousandth time: If no one else was noticing, *was* anything wrong with me?

When the session was over, I got in my car and headed straight to Rich's office. He was standing outside his building waiting for me even though I hadn't called to say I was coming. United in fear, our connection had become supernatural.

"Have you heard anything?" he asked without preamble. In addition to being able to get an immediate MRI booking in Buffalo, they also guaranteed a one-day turnaround for the results.

"No," I said, just as my cellphone rang. It was Dr. Shure's office. They had the results.

"Should I make an appointment to come in?" I asked her.

"Are you close by?"

"Yes."

"Why don't you make your way over right now."

"Oh . . ."

"What's going on?" Rich asked.

I covered the phone. "She wants me to come now."

"Can you do that, Ruth?" the voice on the phone asked me.

"Tell her we're on our way," said Rich.

"We're on our way."

2

Spinal Shock

"Stop, *stop*," I said.

Dr. Shure had been reading the full, lengthy report out loud. After she said the word "tumor," I stopped listening.

"I need to know right now if it's . . . if it's cancer."

Rich gripped my hand. Dr. Shure looked back at the report and spoke slowly. "I am ninety percent certain that it is not cancer."

We both let out a relieved breath.

"But it needs to come out right now."

"Is it big?" I asked.

Dr. Shure looked first at Rich, then at me. "It's big."

•

"I'm driving you home."

We were standing outside the medical building. I felt light and strange, as if my body hadn't caught up to the news yet.

"It's okay," I told Rich.

"I don't want you driving alone."

"I have to call my parents."

"We'll call them when we get home."

"I think I just want to drive home by myself. I'm okay. I really am." I really was. Rich stared at me for a long time. Our heads were pulsing with the same four-beat phrase: *What do I do? What do I do? What do I do?* He came to a decision—my decision—to let me drive home on my own.

"Please don't call anyone from the car."

"What are you going to do now?"

"Take the subway to the office, get my car, and meet you at home."

"But I can drive you!"

He shook his head. "I love you."

It was lunchtime. The street was busy. We were standing in the middle of the sidewalk. People had to keep scooting around us. It was so hot, so humid, but when he put his arms around me we were both bone dry. My arms were stippled with goose bumps.

"Oh my God, Rich."

"I know."

I drove home in complete silence—no radio, no air-conditioning, no open window. My hands clenched the steering wheel. I was sitting so straight my back didn't touch the seat. The only good news was that the kids were still at camp for another two weeks. That bought us time to figure out what to tell them.

I was home in less than ten minutes. I whispered to myself: *Now I'm in the driveway, now I'll get out of the car, now I'll walk up the porch stairs, now I'll unlock the front door.* Once inside, I took a walking tour of the main floor as if I were a real estate agent showing my clients the same rooms over and over again. I paced until Rich arrived, just a few minutes later.

"Did you call your parents yet?"

"I was waiting for you."

I picked up the phone, dialed, and walked around the dining

room table, unable to keep still. My mother picked up on the first ring.

"Ruthie?"

"Yes."

I heard her yell, "LARRY, PICK UP THE PHONE! IT'S RUTHIE!"

"Hello, dear." My father. His voice was calm but I could feel both my parents' frenetic, panicked energy coursing through the line.

"What is it? Tell me," my mother said.

"It's okay." I laughed. "Really, it's okay. I have a tumor."

That was not at all how I meant to tell them. I covered my mouth, worried I might throw up, but I played it real cool, like I was talking a robber into giving me his gun. But my parents had been in the parenting game too long to be fooled by my tone, and I realized, in that moment, that I had never been a good actress— just a lucky one.

"Ruthie, you are going to be fine. Do you hear me?" My mother spoke sternly, as if she were mad at me.

"I know."

"Is Rich there?"

"Right beside me."

"Good. Have you called Joel yet?"

My cousin. One of the heads of orthopedic surgery at a major Toronto hospital.

"Not yet."

"Call him right now and call us back. You're going to be fine!" I heard the crack in her voice before she hung up without saying good-bye. I took note: This is what good parents do—cry behind the curtain, never onstage.

"You don't need to read me the entire report," Joel said, cutting to the chase in the way he has done since we were kids. "Just tell me *where* on your spine it is."

"T3 to T5," I said.

"Well," he said, "it's big but it's not that big."

What the hell did *that* mean? I didn't understand any of it. I had never heard of a spinal meningioma, the technical name of my tumor. The *T* was for thoracic spine—my first MRI several months earlier had skipped that region. The focus then had been on two key spots: my lumbar spine and my brain, the only places where MS lived, the only houses we were looking for. But the MRI in Buffalo widened the scope, scanning my thoracic and cervical spine. The culprit had been hiding right between my shoulder blades.

"Are you sure it's not cancer?" I asked Joel.

"Don't be ridiculous," he said.

Dr. Shure was right. Only in the rarest of cases were meningiomas cancerous.

"Okayallrightokay."

I paced the kitchen floor faster now, keeping careful watch of my feet. If Joel wasn't too worried, I told myself, then I didn't need to be too worried. But then he repeated himself, almost as if he thought I couldn't hear him: "Big, but not *that* big."

I felt a kind of frenzied excitement, my body somehow registering my diagnosis as good news, as if something wonderful had just been revealed to me, as if my world were about to change, as if the next stage of my life was beginning *right now*.

All of this was true; none of it was wonderful.

Within hours, my cousin had phoned and made arrangements for me to meet the following week with his good friend, Dr. Ginsberg, who also happened to be the top neurosurgeon in the city—an amazing stroke of luck since new referrals had to wait six months to see him. But it still meant spending at least the next several days intimately connected to a terrible and insidious—possibly life-changing—tumor on my back. I felt it without actually feeling it every moment of the day. There was no question that it was sneaky—my back didn't even hurt. I pictured it tucked inside my spine, a miniature Quasimodo, pulling on a little string here to make my feet trip, another string there to cause my thighs to freeze, and then tugging on this last, most delicate string, connected to my most private parts, stopping them from feeling anything at all. I had never been so close to something so spiteful.

I wrote cheerful letters to the kids, telling them how busy I had been at work, name-checking my most recent commercial bookings, the visits I'd had with their Bubba and Aunt Fanny, the lunches with my friends, the Miami ribs we were planning on having for their welcome-home dinner in less than two weeks' time. I didn't tell them that I called Rich at work constantly so he could tamp down my—our—growing anxiety, or that every afternoon, to get rid of the day faster, I would close the living room curtains and binge-watch sitcoms while laughing at none of them.

At night, my thoughts clacked like a typewriter, writing and rewriting all the facts that had led me to this point. I called Marc, an old friend who was also a doctor, to help me further decipher my MRI results. Dr. Shure had given me a copy, which I read and reread a thousand times, circling some words, underlining others, scribbling question marks everywhere, looking for clues to my outcome. I was falling into a rabbit hole that I hoped Marc could pull me out of.

"Ruthie," he said, when I called him after midnight one night, "neuralgia is often an impossible thing to get to the bottom of. People get it for no reason and then have to spend the rest of their lives figuring out how to deal with it. You're so lucky to have a definitive diagnosis, and when the surgery is over, you're going to feel just great!"

"You mean everything will go back to normal?" I asked him, trying to nudge my luck more deeply into the good zone. Marc traded in exclamation marks, sprinkling them liberally, like salt, making every bit of bad news taste better.

"Marc?"

In the hesitation that followed, I imagined a world of upbeat possibilities: *you'll feel better than before, you'll run faster, dance better, grow taller, look thinner.*

"Everything will go back to normal, right?"

"You'll feel great," he said. His voice had fallen flat.

I had called him to get the response I wanted, not the one I feared. He, like everyone else, simply could not forecast how my story would end. I was pushing my luck right into a brick wall.

•

I didn't cry—not when I got my diagnosis, not in the days that followed, not before I went to sleep. On a beautiful Wednesday night, the night before my first appointment with Dr. Ginsberg, Rich and I got a seat on a patio in a busy restaurant not far from our house.

"Fuck it," I said, as soon as we sat down. "I'm having a martini."

Rich ordered a beer. There were plenty of pretty people to look at, lots of families strolling with their kids on the sidewalk, ice creams dripping down chubby little hands. The night was warm and breezy. Our drinks came and we clinked glasses but hesitated before making a toast. I looked at Rich. He put his bottle down without saying a word, without taking a sip. His breathing had changed. Rich loves to brag that he never cries.

"Not even when you were little?" I had asked many times. "Not even when you were a baby?"

"Only once. When I was five."

"Oh no! What happened?"

He always shrugs at this point. "I fell down."

His face was crumpling, and then so was mine. I was out of my chair in a flash. I came up behind him and put my arms around his neck.

"It's going to be okay," I said, over and over. We nodded our heads together. Our drinks sat on the table, sweaty and warm, untouched. We paid the bill and left.

•

Rich and I were sitting so close together in the doctor's tiny office at St. Mike's hospital, that I was practically in his lap. "Exactly how long have I been schlepping this tumor around?" I asked Dr. Ginsberg at our appointment, trying to turn my tumor into a joke.

"It appears to be a slow-growing one," he said. "I'd say . . ."

He stopped, considered my feet again. I had just repeated some of the same exercises I had done in Dr. Shure's office. One of them, walking with my feet tightly placed in front of each other, something I'd been able to do just weeks before, was now impossible. Once I had my feet in place, I was stuck. I couldn't move backward or forward. It was as if I were sandwiched between two walls.

"I'll be one moment," Dr. Ginsberg said. "I want to take another look at your MRI."

I watched him walk out of his office, jealous of the way his pigeon-toed feet moved so easily across the floor. When he returned, he sat down and rested his hands on his knees. "Judging from its size, I'd say your tumor has been growing for about ten years."

"Ten years? How did I not *know* this?" I asked him. "Not *feel* it?"

"Because it wasn't interfering with any of your body's functions—until now. In fact, most meningiomas are never discovered. People die without ever having been bothered by their presence."

"How old are you?" I asked.

He smiled before answering. Dr. Ginsberg was bow-legged with reddish hair, a small bearded chin, and kind eyes.

"I'm forty-five."

"May I see your hands, please?"

He held them out in front of me and I watched them long enough to see that, even under close scrutiny, they didn't shake.

"How long have you been a neurosurgeon?"

"Nine years. Ruth, I need to explain to you the risks of this surgery."

Rich and I were holding hands so tightly it was starting to hurt, but neither of us dared let go.

"They are paralysis, death, incomplete tumor resection, spinal cord injury, CSF leak, infection, anesthetic related complications . . ."

I didn't hear anything after he said the words *paralysis* and *death*.

"I want this thing off my back," I said.

"I know."

"When can you do it?"

I braced myself for how long I would have to wait. I was thinking about my kids, who were coming home from camp in just two days; about the shopping I would have to do to get them ready for the school year; about Joey beginning his first year of high school and how I wanted him to transition out of wearing sweatpants every day to wearing skinny jeans to suit his long and lean frame. I was thinking about how *Degrassi* would be resuming production in the next couple of weeks, which meant I would need to slip back into the role of my TV daughter's strong, Christian mother, a mother who didn't have a tumor on her back.

"I can do it on Tuesday," he said. "Four days from now. Is that soon enough?"

I could have cried from both relief and terror and, when we left his office, that's exactly what I did.

•

When I was in my mid-thirties, I had everything I had ever wanted: a man I loved, two little boys, a regular role in a television series, and a monthly column in a fashion magazine. But God help me if I walked past my room and saw a pile of unfolded laundry on the bed. My heart would race. Panic would set in. I would crumple to the floor in a heap—crying, miserable, overwhelmed. But waking after surgery, I was introduced to a whole other level of panic, so beyond my control it felt as if I were being forced to watch my own twisting, writhing body as a reminder that histrionics are reserved for the person who cannot come up with one single significant problem in her life.

The surgery was over, I had been moved out of the recovery room, the tumor had been successfully cut out, but something was still terribly wrong with me. I wiggled my toes—a faint memory dropping in, something about the significance of their movement. But I couldn't move my legs. In fact, I couldn't figure out where my legs were. Did they remove them in surgery? Why could I wiggle my toes but not feel my legs? I struggled to sit but was pulled up short by a bolt of pain in my back. I tried to reach out, to grab on to anything.

I was in a ward with three other patients. The fellow beside me moaned loudly and talked in his sleep. The gentleman in the bed across from me got up, walked to the middle of the room, and peed on the floor while the man diagonally across from me kept trying to escape. He was yelling at the nurses in English, but when that didn't work, he hollered out random French words: "*Monsieur! Soufflé! Bonjour!*" Compared to my comrades, my panic attack seemed almost quaint. Rich's face appeared. He hovered over me, a moon of worry. I locked eyes with him, trying to tell him it was the panic, not the surgery that was killing me. Before I knew what was happening, a nurse wearing impossibly thick glasses shoved an Ativan in my mouth. My tongue was as dry as a slab of brisket. I couldn't generate enough saliva to make it dissolve.

"It's still there." I panted. "Can't swallow it."

"No, no," she said. "It's gone."

Rich looked inside my mouth.

"It *is* there," Rich confirmed. "She needs water."

"It's supposed to dissolve on its own," Nurse Glasses insisted.

"She needs water!" Rich said, and water appeared.

I wanted to ask him: Had the worst happened? Was I paralyzed? He held my chin and gently tipped the water into my mouth. I must have swallowed; it must have worked.

●

It took seven and a half hours for Dr. Ginsberg to remove the meningioma from my spine.

"The most difficult surgery I have ever performed," he told me.

The tumor had snuggled right into my back, happy to not be a bother to anyone until, like a closeted Broadway star, it broke free of its cramped quarters between T3 and T5 and sang in a shattering central nervous system vibrato, *I gotta be me!*

This was not standard meningioma behavior. Meningiomas are easily overlooked because they're not scene-stealers like malignant tumors. They are relatively innocuous looking—egg-shaped with a tiny tail—and are generally easy to peel off whatever tissue they've attached themselves to. My meningioma, however, was as hard as a rock and completely adherent to the dura—the protective lining around my spine. I read this in the Operative Summary that appeared next to my bed soon after I was transferred out of the ward and into a semiprivate room. The words all ran together, a cluster of technical mumbo-jumbo I couldn't begin to comprehend, save for a few notes, like this one: *I called in my colleague for assistance . . . this was a challenging case, and having another pair of hands would assist in improving the patient's quality of outcome.* Together, the two surgeons painstakingly picked at the tumor, knowing every step of the way that if one or the other of them pulled too hard or became too frustrated or too aggressive, they could paralyze me.

When I opened my eyes again, it seemed three days had passed. I should have been going home, but I wasn't going anywhere. I'd forgotten how to walk.

3

Forgetting (How to Pee)

I wasn't paralyzed. This was good news, tremendous news, the best news. And yet, it was almost eerie how no one really talked about it, since, other than death, it was the only thing we had all feared. But something strange had happened to me. My legs were not only *not* paralyzed, they seemed to have surpassed being capable of movement—they had become unhinged. They wandered everywhere of their own volition. I watched with morbid fascination as they slithered off the bed, entangled themselves in the sheets, banged into my tray table, tried to kick my mother in the face as she put on my socks. Completely sidestepping my brain's directives to move only where and when I told them to, they had gone rogue, and I had no idea how to control them. But they were functional. I was so grateful for this piece of good news, I chose not to look too carefully—not to look at all, in fact—at this other bizarre sign of trauma. An untapped resolve had taken shape inside me where curiosity used to exist. I didn't want to know any more than I needed to know. But other people wanted to know. I had to give them more than my loopiness and stubborn ignorance to hold on to. I needed to show them that, on some level, I had control over my circumstances.

So I became obsessed with my bed.

With the exception of Rich, Joey, and Henry, I wouldn't let anyone sit on it. My sheets had to be tightly tucked under the mattress, army-style, with my legs firmly tucked under the sheets at all times. If you leaned your hand on my bed, you were responsible for smoothing over the mess.

"Karen," I said sharply to my sister, after she touched my sheets one visit. "Fix them. Now."

She laughed. I didn't. "Tuck them under. Tighter."

I could see—but not feel—the outline of my toes edging to the corner, searching for any pocket of escape. My bedsheet vigilance also served as a handy distraction from the Operative Summary report that I kept peeking at. Certain phrases had started bobbing to the surface, sharp and dangerous, impossible to shove back down once read: . . . *major dural attachments . . . a large portion of the dura had to be excised . . . which included nerve roots on both sides because they were embedded in the dural-based portion of this tumor . . . concerned about sacrificing the radicular arteries at this level but no choice . . . ended up excising a large portion of the dura . . . necessitated major reconstruction . . . sewed in a dural replacement . . . a challenging case.*

Somehow word had spread that, although the surgery was successful, something was still very wrong with me. I got a panicked email from my friend Michael who had heard from my friend Fli who had heard from our friend Liza who must have heard from my parents or my sisters or Rich, that I was still in hospital, that no one knew when I would be leaving, that I couldn't walk. *I must let Michael know I'm perfect*, I thought. I wrote him back right away:

All is not doom and gloom, I can promise you that. In fact, I have had some of the biggest laughs ever these last few days.

Par example:

Sheryl's daughter, who is seven, asked her if I still had legs.

Henry, after spending several days in Collingwood with my little sister, Jackie, while Rich and I tried to shield the boys from some of the scarier aspects of my diagnosis and imminent surgery, declared that he was having the best week OF HIS LIFE.

And yesterday, Joey said that his friend Ethan passed on his condolences. I said: please tell him I say thank you. And that I'm not dead.

Michael replied within minutes.

I know it's not doom and gloom, but come on, a BIT of gloom is permissible.

I had a dream that you were partway down a cliff, on a ledge, and I was trying to climb down to you. Sad, huh?

"I'm not reading any more emails," I told Rich.

"Let me take care of that," he said. "I'll update everyone, keep people in the loop."

Better them than me, I thought. I was much happier *being* looped than being *in* the loop.

My back was on fire. It felt as if it had been sliced open, which it had. Staples held the top part of it together, an image that made my stomach turn. I hadn't yet tried putting on a bra. I wondered how I would ever manage to get my arms around my back without my back coming apart. Rich and my parents asked the doctors and nurses dozens of questions every time they came in the room—but I was mostly silent. Still, I tried to concentrate on the answers and to write down everything that was said. When I looked at my notes later, most of what I had written was spelled wrong or only half answered. There were whole lines containing only ellipses and question marks. I couldn't think straight, and because Rich was at-tuned to my every cry of pain and sudden panic attack, he couldn't think straight, either.

After one particularly harrowing attack—for which I swal-lowed a double dose of Ativan—my children came to visit—the first time since my surgery. I begged Rich to heave me into the wheelchair—even though I wasn't in any condition to be sitting—so that as many indignities as possible would be hidden from sight. I remembered well Joey's reaction when he saw me in the hospital right after Henry's C-section birth. He squeezed Rich's hand while trying not to stare at the tubes sneaking out from under my sheets. He wouldn't hug me. He smiled, as if to say—*I'm sure you're still very nice but a restraining order might also be very nice.*

Once I was positioned in the chair, Rich hastily tossed a blan-ket across my wandering legs. It was all I could do to keep my pumpkin head up. The kids came in slowly and sat across from me. I was alert enough to register their twin looks of worry and confusion. None of us were prepared for this mess, but as parents with pretty decent instincts, Rich and I had failed to give them enough information. There were things I needed to say, but I was so tired. My eyelashes felt as heavy as velvet curtains.

"Joey, you need to know something," I said, and then paused, lighting on a great idea. I put my elbow on the arm of my chair and then plunked my head on top of it, but then I forgot what it was that I needed Joey to know. My Ativan-addled brain sloshed from side to side while my children looked anywhere but at me. Henry tested out the movability of his mouth, sticking his jaw out and moving it left and right. He picked both feet up and looked at them, put them down, picked them up again, looked at them. The cuddler in the family, even he was wary of getting too close.

"First of all," I said loudly, my head feeling much lighter cupped in my left hand, "this is only temporary. It's true that I can't walk right now but I'm going to be going to rehab for a while and they're going to help me figure it out by me—my? me? no, my, I'm sure it's my—going there."

I looked around the room until my eyes found Rich. Was someone keeping track of how many times I said the word *going*? No one looked too alarmed. I continued. "Joey? Okay?"

"Fine," he said.

"Joe." He looked at me. "Dad and I didn't lie to you. We honestly thought I'd be out of here in three days. Things were just a little more complicated than any of us thought it would be but I'm going to be okey-dokey. Okey-dokey?"

"Fine."

I felt helpless, afraid, and useless, but I was too drained of energy to say anything more. My left hand still holding up my head, I fell asleep before they even left the room.

●

My nervous system had been severely rattled by surgery. My spine was in revolt. I must have been told that the spine likes to be touched about as much as a cat likes a nice hot bath, but I don't remember. I also don't remember hearing about the phenomenon of spinal shock, which occurs almost immediately following surgery and involves the loss of all neurologic activity below the level of injury, which in my case was between my shoulder blades, producing a profound inability to relax the bladder. This bit of news grabbed my attention immediately, diverting thoughts away from my wandering legs and feet.

I couldn't pee. My brain received the message that I needed to, but like a bad receptionist, it held on to the message while it tended to other things.

During the previous five months, I had been stingy with the doctors regarding anything other than my tingly feet, controlling what I believed to be the only path worth pursuing. I should have come clean regarding all my symptoms, but the word *tingles* was so innocuous, so *cute*, it was easier to believe that nothing too onerous could possibly come of it, unlike the other less-cute symptoms—fiery/icy thighs and a bum so suddenly clueless it had trouble maintaining its balance on even the widest of seats. Of course, all my troubles were connected—each symptom plugged into the same switchboard. After the tumor was removed, the sheer volume of unplugged wires was so overwhelming, I decided to focus on the one I assumed to be the easiest to plug back in: peeing on my own.

Several times a day, a nurse came to my room, shooed everyone out, shut the curtains around my bed, and attached an IC—an intermittent catheter—to my urethra. I cried almost every time. I was unable to keep my knees upright while the nurse attached the long plastic tube to me.

"Should I hold my thighs up?" I asked my nurse.

"No need."

She moved quickly, efficiently, without eye contact.

"Do you have children?" I asked.

She sighed heavily. "Yes. A son."

"How old is he?"

"Old enough to know better."

Her hands were steady, but not her voice.

"Has something happened?"

"You don't want to know."

"That doesn't sound good."

I had been holding my thighs up but decided to slowly, slowly pull my hands away, only to watch helplessly as my legs bounced back onto the bed froggy-style. "I told you, you could just let them flop to the sides if you wish." Her voice had grown gentler. She looked at me, waiting for me to say something. What I wanted to say was: *This is* not *what I wish. What I* wish *is that my legs will do what my brain has politely asked them to do, and stay the fuck up.*

Instead, I said, "You seem like a really good mom."

"Thank you." She smiled at me.

"You have such nice hair," I told the next nurse.

"What a sweetie you are!" she said.

To another nurse: "I've always wanted to go to Greece. Tell me what it's like."

And another: "I said well-done, not dead!" And she laughed and laughed.

And another: "Do you think I'll walk again?" No answer.

The next one: "You sound like an amazing cook."

And later: "I can't believe you stole me a muffin!"

And the next: "You're my favorite."

After each nurse left, all I could think about was my next IC and how much it scared me—not because of what it did for me but because of what it meant I couldn't do for myself. It was as if my brain and my sacral nerves had had a huge fight and were now giving each other the silent treatment. Peeing on my own was proving to be as easy as climbing a mountain with no legs.

I was facing two equally plausible possibilities: Either my peeing problem would resolve itself in six weeks or so, around the time spinal shock starts to ease up, or there would be no resolution, necessitating the use of a catheter for the rest of my life. Had I known the extent to which my entire nervous system had been shaken, I would have felt powerless, but my ignorance proved to be a lucky break.

A woman hugging several grainy brown files, spilling over with paper, came to see me one morning.

"You're going to be transferred to Lyndhurst," she said, "a spinal rehab facility, but we don't know when." She looked exhausted. "They don't have any room right now."

"Okay." I couldn't think of a single question to ask her.

"What do you mean, you don't know when?" Rich asked, rising from his seat. "Days? Weeks?"

"I really don't know. When a bed becomes available, she'll be moved."

"Are there no other rehab facilities in the city? No other place she can go? She doesn't know how to walk!"

"We will have her moved as soon as possible, I promise."

"We're going to the States," Rich said, once she left. "I want to speak to Joel. This is insane. You can't just stay here in the hospital indefinitely until some bed turns up for you. You've been here over a week already! How long are we supposed to wait? I don't care how much it costs—we're going to the States."

We got in touch with Joel, who did an admirable job of calming Rich down. "They'll find her a room at Lyndhurst soon," he said. "Don't worry, Rich."

But it was all Rich could do. Worrying was his new job. I was also worried, but for a different reason. The nurses had told me only the day before that once I went to rehab, I would likely have to learn how to catheterize myself. That was never going to happen. I now had my first post-surgery goal: to pee like a normal person.

Rich had been with me every day and every night, sleeping in the visitor's lounge. Sometimes he was lucky enough to get the long couch to himself; other nights he slept on two chairs pushed together. He never once complained. But I needed him to leave for a few hours. I had hatched a plan and wanted to surprise him the following morning with the outcome.

Enter Fli—one of my closest friends—with a huge order of sushi and several bottles of water. Fli and I had been roommates when we were both struggling actresses. What we "struggled" with then made us *baha* with laughter now: for me, what boys to kiss;

for her, what girls to kiss. It was a glorious angst-filled time with nothing more pressing to focus on than our (relatively) flat-bellied navels. Now, with a little life under our belts, we both knew what struggle meant. But things were about to get better. My plan had three simple components: eat a little, drink a lot, pee. What could be easier? I could sense Fli's struggle not to Google, right in front of me, how best to do this. Her legendary attention to detail was why she was the perfect scene-study partner when we were both students in theater school: She did all the work, I did all the eating. But I didn't need Google to tell me that the best way to empty a bladder was to fill it first.

Enter Archie. The most gorgeous, hot male nurse I'd ever seen. I told him my plan while Fli and I ate and drank and drank and drank.

"It takes a little more time than that to get things moving," he said, his arms flexing without him even trying. I was still blissfully unaware of the massive understatement contained in the words *a little more time*. What he meant was possibly weeks, months, years, never. But I couldn't even begin to see that then.

Eight o'clock and eight cups of water later, I kicked Fli out and prepared myself for the miracle that was all set to happen right there in the acute care unit of St. Mike's hospital.

"Archie," I said. "Let's do this thing." I held up a warning hand. "But I'll need a female nurse, please. No offense."

That was my first mistake.

Getting back and forth to the washroom was a production no one looked forward to, which was why it was as easy to hail a nurse as it was a hedgehog. Just that afternoon, in earlier fruitless attempts to use the washroom, Milena, the Christian Rasta Care Assistant who came when I buzzed, had her hands full. Transferring back to my bed from the wheelchair proved a Herculean task. I kept apologizing for being useless; she kept apologizing for having such skinny arms. With a lot of huffing and puffing, I managed to get my whole top half, including my uncooperative bum—which couldn't tell the difference between a chair and air—onto the bed, but my legs dangled precariously over the edge and I couldn't lift them up on my own. The only way I wouldn't slide off the bed altogether was if Milena threw herself on top of me and fastened me there with her lanky body, which, shockingly, was exactly what she did. We were both breathing heavily, our noses touching, and then we burst out laughing. Milena grabbed the sides of my head with her latex-gloved hands and planted a kiss on my forehead. *Praise Jesus.*

But that night, for my first round trip to the washroom, two nurses arrived in record time and, with as much help from me as I could offer, flipped me onto the commode and rolled me to the washroom, where I peed with very little drama. It would appear that not only had my experiment worked, but it was over. So much for Archie and his doubtful attitude.

10:20 P.M. I had to pee again. No nurse to be found.

11:10 P.M. Still needed to pee, felt quite desperate. Then, Carlito came.

"I'll look away," he said, as I tried to pull down the Depends my poor father was conscripted to buy in case my bladder ever decided to start without me. I held a little towel across my lap for modesty.

"Hold this, please," I said, passing it to him to shield us from each other like we were Jewish orthodox newlyweds about to get down for the first time. I managed to pee again, but not nearly enough. My belly was sloshed. This run of male nurses was throwing me off my game.

11:40 P.M. I had to pee again. The need was so desperate, so crazed, I feared I was losing my mind. No matter how hard I pressed that buzzer, no one came.

Everything I'd ever heard or read about the dearth of nurses in our health care system was true. I had been surviving because I knew how to joke and to ask the nurses questions about themselves. I knew how to pretend that the only reason I was there was to tell them how pretty they were or how well they did their job or what a great parent they must be. I made them laugh, and Rich told me how much they loved me. Even in the hospital, *especially* in the hospital, I needed that love: Love represented the golden ticket. I puffed them up in the hopes of getting a shower or someone to lift me out of my bed and onto the commode. In prison, cigarettes or ramen noodles might have done the trick; here, my only currency was charm, but as the night wore on with no relief or sleep in sight, my charm well was running dry in direct inverse proportion to my waterlogged belly.

I pressed the buzzer with heedless abandon, not caring how grating the sound must have been at the nurses' station.

Archie finally returned. We eyed each other as though ready to draw our guns. He was there to do exactly what I needed him to do, exactly what his job *required* him to do, which was to stick the damn catheter in me and drain me, motherfucker. But I wouldn't let him.

"I can do it," he said.

"No. I need someone else."

"There *is* no one else," he said, frustration pulsing in a vein on the side of his bald head.

"Please find someone else," I said. "Find someone else, Archie! Go! Find someone else! Find someone else! Go! Go now! Go!"

He went.

When I am like this at home, my son Henry will get very quiet and then shake his head and mutter "*Crazy lady*" under his breath. I knew the only person I was hurting was myself, but I insisted that a woman and not a man touch my hoo-ha, even if it was a hoo-ha I could barely feel. I cupped my belly with both hands. The darkness of the room did nothing to mitigate my misery. A while later, I pressed the buzzer again and Archie returned.

"No one has come yet?" he asked, his face still beautiful, but distressed.

I shook my head.

He pointed to himself with a raised eyebrow: *Are you ready to allow me to do my job now?*

I shook my head.

He sighed, then dragged what looked like an ultrasound machine on wheels my way.

"At the very least, I have to check," he said.

"Check what?"

"What level you're at."

He rubbed gunk on my stomach and then waved the wand around it. When he saw what he needed to see, he stepped back and clasped his hands over his head and puffed out his cheeks.

"What?" I asked him.

"This is bad."

"What's bad?" I said.

"When you're at five hundred milliliters, we *have* to drain you."

"What am I at?" I asked.

"Over a thousand."

No comment.

"Just let me do it."

"No."

"Please. I have to do an IC. I have no choice." He was pleading with me, but I didn't care.

"Get someone else."

Amazingly, Archie left the room. A few minutes later, Ethel showed up. She moved like a slow yawn. Maybe they had drawn sticks at the nurses' station to see who would get stuck with me.

Ethel had lost. She snapped her latex gloves on, then tried to turn on the light clamped to my bed.

"It doesn't work!" I screamed. I didn't care if I woke up my roommate on the other side of the curtain. "Just turn on the big light, the *big* light!"

I couldn't remember the word for *overhead*. Ethel stopped what she was doing to get a better look at me. I immediately shut up. The pain in my bladder was so extreme, I couldn't afford to have her leave. But I also felt sorry for her: Who could possibly like working the graveyard shift and being yelled at by a pregnant lady *who wasn't even pregnant?*

"Please," I begged her, in my softest, most-likely-to-be-mistaken-for-sane voice. "Please, just turn on the big light and do the IC. The other patient won't wake up, I promise," I said.

She didn't say a single word. I searched her eyes for some kind of softness as she inserted the catheter, but she just looked forward at a spot high above my head. We both listened as an endless stream of my pee poured into the big square of hospital-issue Tupperware; I filled it to the very top. She took the catheter out and pulled my Depends back up. Then she lifted the Tupperware with two hands, grunted, and left. No temperature check, no blood pressure check, no "good night."

But just like that, my mood, as well as my entire body, felt eight pounds lighter. I loved everybody again—even Ethel.

"Thank you so much!" I called out, but she was gone.

4

Forgetting (How to Be)

Even though I didn't like anyone touching my bed, I also didn't want to be left alone. Ever. My body was a stranger to me, a scary stranger, so I made sure that I had company almost all the time. My guest list was a tightly edited group: my two best friends, my two children, my two sisters, my two parents, and Rich. But on one particularly wretched Sunday morning, five or six days after my surgery, my acting agent unexpectedly appeared outside my room. Rich and I both yelled, "No!" when we saw her. Poor Jennifer backed right out, but not before glimpsing how small and unkempt and sad I was. Although Jennifer and I had enjoyed a great working relationship for eleven years and often spent as much time talking about our families as we did about my future employment, I would never dare make an appearance at my agency without projecting my potential as the fittest forensic psychiatrist/vice principal/assistant DA/mother with a dark past/uptight librarian ever. Jennifer's surprise visit forced Rich and I to close ranks. My husband became not only my tear wiper and social convener, but also my bodyguard.

That same afternoon, my son Henry asked, "Can I lie down next to you?"

I was fine with this, but Rich wasn't. I think he thought my body parts had been replaced with glass.

"I have an idea," Henry said. "You close your eyes and I'll poke you and you tell me if you can feel it."

"All right," I said brightly, as if this were a great idea. "Go for it."

I snuck a quick peek at Joey before closing my eyes. He was staring into his phone, pretending he wasn't sitting in a hospital room where his mother was lying in bed in the middle of the day. Henry started high up, poking me around my rib cage.

"Felt it!"

I tried to shift higher up the bed as I realized I still hadn't worn a bra since I'd been there. I couldn't imagine how I ever would again. Where would the bra sit on my back? Would it snag on the staples? Were the staples there permanently? How many staples were there? I couldn't ask, wouldn't ask. I didn't want to know.

"Mom? Didn't you feel that?"

"Of course I did!"

I had no idea what he had just touched.

"I'll go lower," he said.

"Sure!"

I started cheating, opening my eyes just a touch to gauge where he was poking. I could see he was poking my left thigh, which I still couldn't feel, still couldn't understand where it was.

"Scoot around to this side, honey."

"Why?"

"I'm just more comfortable with you on my right side."

He considered climbing over me in bed but quickly got down and walked around when he saw the look on Rich's face. He snuggled back in.

"Keep going," I said.

He poked my right leg above the knee.

"I fully felt that!" Oh, thank the heavens, I really did.

There was no activity for a few seconds—at least none that I could feel.

I opened my eyes. Henry was looking at me expectantly. Oh, no. I must not have felt what he touched. I was saved from having to explain myself when the doctor came in on his rounds. He politely asked Henry to move so he could examine me. Henry jumped off the bed, grabbed a pencil from my tray table, stabbed my foot, then flopped into a chair and looked hard at the wall.

"Henry!" I said, shocked. "Did you just stab me?"

He dropped his little head in his hands. "Oh, thank God you felt that!"

•

During daylight hours, no one knew which me they would get when they walked into my room. In a way, I had never felt more alive. I was okay. The worst hadn't happened. I hadn't died. I wasn't paralyzed. I focused on all the good things: my back was ravaged yet intact; I still couldn't tell where my feet were but I could see with my eyes that they were there; my stomach was horribly bloated but I had no appetite and was barely eating so surely it would go down eventually. I was incapable of turning over in bed or pulling myself up or sitting without assistance, but that couldn't possibly be considered unusual after spinal cord surgery, could it? A lovely halo of positivity followed me wherever I went, which wasn't far. I had heard stories about people becoming hyper—or manic—after surgery. My mother's friend, after a hip operation, was caught having an intense conversation with two belts. I wasn't quite that far gone, but I was indeed coasting on a high—possibly facilitated by the lingering effects of the anesthesia, plus the morphine, or maybe the switch to oxycodone or the switch again to Percocet. People around me reasonably expected me to feel upset and scared all the time, afraid for my future self. *But I'm happy*, I wanted to tell them, *you have to believe me.* From where they were standing, I didn't seem to be the most reliable judge of my own happiness.

At any given hour, I might bawl my eyes out, hyperventilate, laugh hysterically, go bananas over the deliciousness of a peach, weep with love for my children, marvel at the softness of my pajamas, hide my eyes from the sight of everyone, gossip about my roommate with whom I barely spoke, or flirt with Dr. Ginsberg. One day, when Dr. Ginsberg came to see me, I asked him, "So, will I ever walk again?" My overall dopiness made the most serious question I had ever asked another human being sound as nonchalant as an inquiry into the weather.

Dr. Ginsberg raised his hand and then slowly lowered it as if he were pushing down a French coffee press—measured, careful.

"I feel," he said slowly, "very confident"—pressing a little lower—"that there will be a good"—a little lower still—"outcome." It wasn't the definitive answer I was hoping for, but I was just woo-woo enough not to notice. Any signs of bad news merely floated over my head like tiny little opalescent bubbles, easily popped and forgotten.

And then there was the washcloth incident.

Because virtually every bit of business was conducted from my bed—my ICs, eating, examinations—it also meant I did my morning and evening ablutions there. Rich gallantly took on these duties. In the morning, he would bring the bone-shaped plastic tray to my bed and hold it under my chin while I brushed my teeth, and then bring me a glass of water so I could swish and spit into it. (I only spat on his hand once.) He would also bring a little dish of soapy water and a scratchy hospital washcloth for me to wash my face. But one day, he had a surprise for me.

"You are going to be so happy," he said.

"Oh, yeah?"

"I found the best washcloth ever."

"Okay."

He pulled it out of his bag. "Check it out!" he said. "Touch it. Seriously, just touch it. It's the softest thing you've ever felt, right?"

I looked at it for a long time. It was orange. I touched it. It was soft and nubby.

"Where did you get this?" I asked.

"That's the best part! I found it right under the kitchen sink! I don't know why I've never seen it before. Or why it was there. Actually, why do you put the washcloths under the kitchen sink?"

"Rich!" I yelled. "This isn't a washcloth! It's a Swiffer! I use it to clean the goddamn floor!" I threw it at him. He stood there, holding the Swiffer washcloth, looking confused. "You almost made me wash my face with a *shmata*!" Then I burst into tears.

But something quickly changed. I had been so certain that crying was the right response to this terrible situation; however, when I looked at Rich again, I saw that he was trying not to laugh, which made me laugh, and then we both couldn't stop laughing.

"But you have to admit," he said, "it *is* pretty soft."

At night, I found very little amusing. Often, I would slam into wakefulness. It was always the same routine: I would throw off the covers in a sweat, wondering where my legs were. Gone. Meanwhile, the right foot—also the same size and shape as mine—would be painfully wedged between the food tray and the bed. "Stay," I'd tell my left foot while I pulled the dead weight of my right foot back to bed and gave it a stern warning: Now *don't move*.

No sooner would I position my left leg than it would wander off again like it had had its bell rung one too many times. As strange and frustrating as it was to play this game of hide-and-seek with my own body parts, when the sun came up it seemed a lot funnier. When Rich and my parents arrived for their daily duties, I would report on all the places where I'd found my feet in the night. They would listen and laugh, but I could tell they didn't find my stories as funny as I did. They were scared. And the truth was: So was I. None of us knew what the endgame was.

One evening, my cousin Joel came to check on me long after visiting hours were over. Somehow he'd managed to skip right past Rich's bodyguard presence in the hallway. He whooshed the curtains open around my bed and threw the covers off my legs.

"Joel!" I yelled. "You can ask first!"

He stared at my cockeyed feet.

"Let's see you walk," he said, pulling up a chair at the end of my bed, ready for the show to begin.

"I can't."

"What do you mean you 'can't'?"

"What do you mean what do I mean? I *can't* walk."

He sighed, then stood up again, raised his hands, palms facing my feet. "Press them against my hands and start bicycling."

I lifted both my legs at the same time, ignoring the ripping sensation down my spine, and concentrated hard on getting them to stop waving around. After an alarmingly long time, I got both feet onto his palms. That was it. I had to stop for a breather.

"Move them," Joel commanded.

"I need a minute!"

"Go!"

My feet moved like the wheels on a wonky grocery cart.

"Oh," I said. "My God." It was the first time I realized how bad my coordination was.

A shadow moved across Joel's face. He understood something I didn't.

"What?" I asked.

"That's why you can't walk."

"Why?"

"Proprioception."

"Huh?"

"Your legs don't know where they are in space."

This made no sense to me. And then, just like that, it was the *only* thing that made sense to me. It answered the question my body had been asking for months: *Where the fuck are you?*

"Will it go away?" What I meant was: *Will my legs ever know where they are again?*

He thought about this, a few possibilities running through his mind. "We'll see," he said. "You'll be in rehab longer."

Longer? Longer than *what*? Word had come down: A room was available at Lyndhurst. Some paperwork needed to be done, arrangements for transfer made, and in two or three days I would be leaving. But how much longer was I going to be away from my family? How long, exactly, would rehab take? I didn't ask. Instead, I squeezed my eyes shut and took a second to shove the panic back down my throat. "I don't quite get this."

Joel sighed.

"The tumor was sitting on your proprioceptive nerve, which is the nerve that tells your body where it is in space. It's like the other sense, the sixth one."

My legs and feet had amnesia. I could only assume my bum was in the same boat.

"But there's good news," Joel said. "Didn't I tell you that if you were able to move your toes after surgery, everything would be okay?"

"That reminds me. One doctor who does rounds—*not* my beloved Dr. Ginsberg," I told Joel. "I can't remember his real name so I just refer to him as Dr. Asshole." Villains were hard to come by at St. Mike's—if they were there at all—but I needed one. I chose him. "Anyway, he does the toe test on me every morning. I close my eyes and I have to tell him if my toes are moving up or down.

I have no clue. I fail every time. It's like grade-eleven math all over again."

I was more disturbed by this than my light tone suggested. Although I *saw* my toes moving, I couldn't actually *feel* them moving.

"I texted Howard." Joel said.

"During my surgery?"

"Right after. I'll show you."

He came to the side of my bed and scrolled through their many text exchanges. Most if not all the texts revealed my cousin's need to know if my toes were moving, his messages taking on greater urgency as time went on. *Well? Are they moving? Yes or no? Are they?* I could feel the tension in Dr. Ginsberg's replies. *I don't know yet. She hasn't woken up, Joel.* They could have been college students tracking the progress of a friend whom they were responsible for getting hammered the night before. I looked up at my cousin. He was four years older than me and more than a foot taller. He didn't always have patience for people, but for some reason he has always had a soft spot for me.

"You were worried about me," I said.

He put his phone back in his pocket and sat down as if he hadn't heard.

•

After I'd spent four or five days in the hospital, almost all of it lying down, Dr. Asshole told me I needed to start spending more time out of bed, sitting up. So one morning, when my sister Karen and my girlfriend Sheryl came to visit, I sat up. Karen had just finished telling me that, as per Rich's and my request, she had found and interviewed a wonderful nanny named Ellen who was willing to help the boys and Rich at home, and could start right away. I was so relieved to hear this. Ellen would pick up Henry from school and be there to make dinners and clean up and hang out with the kids until Rich returned from work. I wanted to find out more, but sitting was hard work. I was feeling light-headed and clammy. Karen and Sheryl were talking about something and I was trying to listen, but I felt sweat dripping from my neck and back. There was a massive dead spot on my spine where I felt nothing. I needed to lie down, but didn't want to interrupt the conversation. The buzzing in my entire lower half was relentless. I glanced at my phone—I'd been sitting up for only ten minutes, which was already eight minutes too long. I had the sense one of my feet—I wasn't sure which one—was caught under something. One of my knees was waving. It was as if a beast was awakening under the covers.

"I have to lie down," I blurted out. "I'm so sorry!"

Karen and Sheryl leapt to their feet and quickly flagged down a nurse who helped me back to bed. Visiting hour was officially over.

Each day after that, I was able to sit up a little longer, until finally, Rich took me for my first walk outside. I hadn't felt the sun on my face since before I came into the hospital. That was near the end of August. It was now the end of the first week of September. Normally I hide from the sun, having taken all the warnings about its treachery firmly to heart, but on this day I rolled along with my face tipped rebelliously upward. The sidewalks were bumpy in a way I'd never noticed before. The plan was to get to the diner diagonally across from the hospital, but the streetcar tracks proved prohibitive. We took the road straight ahead, with Rich clumsily negotiating my wheelchair over all the cracks and curbs. We felt like champs when we finally reached the glassy café. There were two charming little tables out front. Rich parked me in the sun, but there was still a slice of shade to dip into if needed. I was showing Rich how I could move my ankles up and down. My right foot looked pretty straight, but my left foot veered out like there was something it really needed to see over there.

Next to our table was a young woman. She looked like she might have been a street kid once. She was wearing oversized button earrings, the kind that enlarge the hole to frightening proportions; a horseshoe ring through her nose; pink hair poking out from under her little po'boy cap; and a patchwork maxi dress. Her sad, tidy father was with her, drinking his Starbucks and smoking the last bit of his cigarette.

"I'm just watching what you're doing," she said. "That was exactly what I used to do. Are you going to Lyndhurst for rehab?" she asked.

"I am."

"Oh, you're going to absolutely love it!"

"Actually," I said, "I'm going to love going home."

Her father nodded when I spoke, as if I was the only person who understood why people went to rehab: not to love it, but to leave it.

"I guess you have a spinal cord injury, too?" she asked.

"Oh, no. Nothing like that." I said. "I had this thing on my back but it's gone now."

She nodded. "They all have SCIs at Lyndhurst."

I looked at Rich. "I'm sorry?" I said. "I don't know what that is."

"SCI," she said slowly. "Spinal. Cord. Injury."

My stomach reacted while my brain struggled to keep up. "But I don't have one of those," I said. "My problem is gone. I'm all better. Just, well, I can't walk right now is all."

"At Lyndhurst, they taught me how to walk again. But I can't go very far. Just from, say, here to inside there." She pointed with her head to the café beside us. Then she added with a triumphant smile, "I can't feel my feet!"

I needed to get away from this girl. She kept talking. "You'll probably get either Neil or Amanda for physio. I had Neil. He's *awesome*. Physio is mandatory at Lyndhurst—no skipping! Everything else is optional. You can do yoga, go swimming, tons of stuff. You'll love it!"

Like I was going to a country club for the wheelchair set. The phrase *well-heeled* popped into my head and then, just as quickly, *no-heeled*.

Rich picked up on my cues and rolled me back to the hospital, away from the punky girl and her sad father. Even though I couldn't walk, had no control over my bladder or bowels, had trouble sitting up, needed painkillers, couldn't keep track of my legs, and could barely feel my feet, I was fine. I was not an SCI person. The tumor was gone. I was obviously okay.

My happy story and manic phase were about to come to a crashing end.

PART TWO

next steps

5

My New Life in Rehab

After nine long days, I was finally leaving the hospital, but I couldn't fathom how. I woke up early on the day of my discharge. Nurse Theresa washed me while I lay in bed and whimpered like a toddler. I just wanted to wash myself, standing up, in a shower, alone.

Rich was at home getting the boys ready for their first day back to school. Even though I hate making lunches, I would have given my left baby toe, which was now useless, just to assemble Joey's baggie of cereals—the only lunch he has eaten for the last six years—and to make Henry's nitrate-free roast turkey sandwich with Swiss cheese and mayonnaise. Would Rich remember to give them each a piece of fruit, and something salty and something sweet? It had been a while since I had left them an embarrassing note inside their lunchboxes on the first day back to school, but I would have made a point of it this year—Joey's first in high school, Henry's last in elementary.

While Theresa washed my hair, my thoughts circled back to just ten days earlier, the night before my surgery. Arrangements were made for the boys to sleep out, since Rich and I had to leave so early the following morning. While they were gone, I left them each a note on their pillow telling them how proud I was of them, how funny and smart they both were. I said that I loved them, but was careful to write it only once so as not to betray my own fears. I didn't specify when I would see either of them again. As I wrote, I tried not to think of them at ages eighteen and twenty-five and forty. I resisted the urge to make any one sentence too heavy with meaning, even if the worst happened and I died on the operating table and they felt compelled to forever after carry my notes around, parsing each sentence for hidden meaning, asking over and over: *Did she know she would die? And if she did, couldn't she have said something more profound than, "Don't forget your lunchbox at school"?*

My hair washed, Theresa slowly dried it so as not to jostle me too much. I could have wept all over again at the gentle care she took with me, which led me to thoughts of Rich and how we had woken up in the dark the day of the surgery. I had taken a shower—what would be my last one standing up for a long time—then asked Rich to rub down my back with the two antiseptic sponges I had been given at the hospital the week prior—the incision area needed to be as clean as possible. I had dried my hair. No makeup, no moisturizer, no smile. Before we left the house I checked inside my purse to make sure the card I had secretly written for Rich was there. I grabbed my overnight bag, turned on the house alarm, and clicked the door shut. The drive downtown was quick and quiet. I sat hunched in my seat, all my muscles clenched. Rich sat as straight as I had ever seen him sit, his hands in the perfect 10-2 position on the steering wheel. In the parking lot, before we left the car, I put my hand over his.

"I wrote you a card. It's in my purse." I started to cry. "Don't open it unless you have to."

"Don't talk like that," he said, squeezing my hand back but still looking straight ahead.

"Unless you have to," I said again.

Once I was lying on the stretcher, things moved so quickly I scarcely had time to process. My clothes were removed upon arrival and transferred into a plastic bag marked "Personal Belongings." Rich kissed me good-bye, as did my parents and sister Karen—my little sister, Jackie, was out of town keeping Henry distracted, while Joey was being distracted at my girlfriend Sheryl's house. Rich kissed me again and then turned away and looked at the wall, his palms together, fingertips pressed against his lips.

"Honey, it's going to be okay," I said as they wheeled me into the OR, my arm stretching back behind me. "It's going to be okay!"

In the OR, everyone was extremely busy. It was almost an excited atmosphere, expectant, like they were all waiting for the guest of honor at a surprise birthday party. The special guest turned out to be the neurosurgeon, Dr. Ginsberg. He came in last and stroked my arm. He smiled at me. That's the last thing I remember.

And now Nurse Theresa was done with my hair. She busied herself tidying up my room, getting me ready for my transfer to Lyndhurst. I didn't have much—just my "Personal Belongings," which now included my bag, my notebook, and some magazines. I checked inside my purse to see what was left in there: my cell phone, an explosion of Kleenex, my lip balm, and the card I had written for Rich, unopened.

"Tell me your story," I said to Theresa as she finished up. One thing I'd learned while being in hospital: no questions were off limits, even when—*especially* when—they were personal. The nurses couldn't tell me when I was going to walk again or if I would ever feel my legs the way I used to, but they could tell me, under cover of night, that their partner was doing time for bringing cocaine into their home country but that he also never forgot their daughter's birthday. They could tell me about their recent honeymoon. They could tell me how much they missed home and their families living so far away.

That day, Theresa told me her story. She was single, had previously worked as a nanny, had sponsored her sisters to come to Toronto, and wanted to go back to school. She asked me where I lived and when I told her, she clapped her hands with delight.

"I know that area so well!" she said. "I love the challah bread." She pronounced it *kalla*. "And the ladies all run. They love to run. To be sexy!"

When the weather was good, I'd pop my headphones on and zip my cell phone into my jacket pocket and run along the Beltline. I passed dozens of other fit women who were running just as hard, maybe to get themselves into the dress they'd been coveting at Holt Renfrew, or to get the young barista they'd been coveting since their divorce, or to look fine for their high school reunion where they were sure to see the guy they had lost their virginity to. We all wanted different things, but we all wanted to look hot while we chased them.

Theresa left and two paramedics and a rolling bed appeared in my room. According to the weather icon on my phone, it was a hot one outside, but the men were still dressed in heavy gear. Their enormous boots announced: *We are men and we are here to take care of you.* In one swift motion I was transferred from my bed onto their wheeled one. I protested lightly when they put the seatbelt around my waist, even though I was lying down.

"No need," I said. "I promise not to hurl myself off."

What I didn't say was that my bum might have other plans, but it wouldn't have mattered anyway. They joked with me, but the seatbelt stayed fastened. I looked straight up into their handsome faces and knew why women fantasized about paramedics. They had thick arms and good hair and easy smiles. I bantered with them in the elevator and kept it going while they transferred me into the back of the ambulance. I talked while they slammed the back doors shut. We drove out of the dark underground and into the light of day, and I blinked several times before I abruptly stopped talking. A massive knot had formed in my chest. I was terrified. Somehow, impossibly, I had grown used to being in the hospital. I knew what being in the hospital meant. I had a routine, I knew the nurses, I understood shift changes and IC protocol and who best to coax into washing my hair.

I had no idea what this next move meant.

I clutched my purse and pulled my chin down. I could see my chest bouncing with the effort not to start its staccato rhythm—a clear sign the knot was about to come loose, that the tears were about to come gushing out.

"Hey, Pete!" the paramedic on my left said, either ignoring or reacting to what was happening to me—I couldn't tell which. "Remember that doctor in the synagogue last year?"

"The one who was having a heart attack but refused our help?" Pete said.

"Yeah, that one."

Then Pete said to me, as if I hadn't heard, "This guy was having a heart attack, wouldn't let us help. His wife calls us from the synagogue, it was a big holiday, the one where everyone goes."

"Rosh Hashanah?" I said.

Pete looked up at the ceiling of the truck, thinking. "The other one."

"Yom Kippur?"

"Yeah! That one! So his wife calls nine-one-one, 'cause her husband's not looking so good, and we get there and he's a *heart* surgeon and he's obviously having what we call a 'walking heart attack' and he refuses our help! We couldn't even believe it, right, Kyle?"

"Unbelievable," Kyle said, shaking his head.

I must have said something to trigger this story, but I couldn't imagine what.

"Guys," I said. "I'm sorry, but I really have to cry now."

Kyle put his hand on my arm the same way Dr. Ginsberg had right before the surgery. It unlocked an even deeper well of tears inside me. I scrunched my face hard to stop them, but all the tears ran out. The guys looked down at their laps while I cried. The ambulance stopped frequently and turned easily and I had no idea where we were. The last time I had lain down in the back of a moving vehicle was when I was a little girl and my parents drove my sisters and me to Grand Island, New York, for a family weekend getaway. We never wore seat belts. We'd sprawl out in the backseat, feet all over each other, playing games.

The ambulance slowed down as it went over two speed bumps, and then came to a full halt.

"Well, Ruth," Pete said, "this is where we leave you."

They rolled me out the back and I heard the long steel legs of the gurney collapse and land with a little bounce on the ground. I was embarrassed to be entering any environment this way— prone, on a rolling bed, covered in a blanket, fastened into place, clutching my purse to my chest. As we entered the facility, I kept my eyes trained on the square tiles above my head, playing a game called: *If I Can't See Them Then They Can't See Me*. We moved as one unit—Kyle, Pete, and me—into an elevator and up to another floor where a battalion of people were standing by to greet me: a nurse, a doctor, a resident, my mom, Rich.

"Where am I?" I asked Rich.

"Lyndhurst."

"I know, but *where*. *Where* is this?"

We were five minutes away from our very first house, which meant five minutes away from where the tumor likely first started to grow on my spine—slowly, masterfully, life-changingly. I was working so hard not to fall apart, I'm not sure I remembered my manners long enough to say good-bye to the paramedics or hello to this new set of medics. I briefly wondered why my mother was there and not my father, and then I wondered why my mother was there at all. Rich carefully helped me get settled into the wheelchair sitting right next to the gurney that the paramedics now wished to repossess. Perhaps to mitigate how overwhelming this transfer into a new environment was for me, I was directed first to the cafeteria to relax and get something to eat.

There were two big-screen TVs on the wall, one tuned to the Food Network, the other to CNN. An A-frame board stood inside the door with the day's menu unevenly scrawled on it in yellow chalk. Four large windows surrounded the cafeteria but only two had a view to the outside, where I could see a gazebo that doubled as a smoker's hut and a huge expanse of lawn intersected by paved walkways and scattered picnic tables. The other two windows overlooked the wide lobby with the truncated cafeteria that served chips and prepackaged salads and sandwiches for visitors and other bipeds.

My mother pushed me in the wheelchair. Even though the appropriate staff had my written medical story, they needed to assess me in person to see what kind of wheels I required. The chair I was given in the meantime was too big. The back was too high, the seat too high, the arms too high; I looked like a Lilliputian.

In the time it had taken me to be transported to Lyndhurst, the dregs of my post-surgery mania were fully flushed out of my system. There was no joy to be found. There was no funny. Nothing would ever be funny again. I regarded my legs balefully, as if I were locked in battle with them. I blamed them for being a couple of idiots and they blamed me for ignoring the distress flares they'd been firing for the five months prior to my diagnosis. I decided to end the détente right then and there. I gently lifted my legs, one at a time, and placed my feet on the footrest, taking the pressure off my thighs. Within seconds, they wandered off again without my noticing and the tips of my sneakers caught under the wheels, making the chair stop abruptly and my mother and I lurch suddenly forward. I clenched my jaw, reached down, and very deliberately put my feet back on the footrest. We pushed on.

There were only a few stragglers in the cafeteria. Lunch service was over but a man in a hairnet and a thick gold chain—I would learn that this was Neville—came rushing over to greet me. He strongly suggested that I order the stir-fry without even referencing the other lunch choices written on the chalkboard. He offered to get my mother a plate even though she was clearly a guest.

"I'm sure you would like to join your daughter," he said, leaning forward with his hands behind his back like he was the maître d' of a fancy restaurant.

"I absolutely would! Thank you so much!"

"It is my pleasure," he said, and then added, apropos of nothing, "I also have apples if you would like to take them to your room after."

My mother fussed to get my chair squared comfortably with the table.

"Stop it!" I snapped at her. "I can do it myself!"

Rich was on his cell phone in the doorway with his head down. I watched him approach our table, but he didn't end his call.

Neville brought us our plates of food. I didn't know what to make of them. There was soy sauce mixed with something orange seeping out from under exhausted-looking vegetables.

My mother made sounds of yumminess as she chewed and chewed. "This is really good," she said.

I clunked down my fork and stared at her, but she wouldn't look at me. I stabbed at my food without eating it. Rich veered away from us, still on the phone, pacing the room. His voice was getting louder and louder. I couldn't figure out who on earth he was yelling at. Rich is a charmer. As a talent agent, he works hard to smooth feathers, not ruffle them. He has a deep, silky voice and an easy laugh, neither of which were on display as he crisscrossed the room, holding the phone away from his ear so he could yell directly into it. My mother looked alarmed; she'd never seen this side of Rich.

"He needs to yell at someone," I said. "So let him yell."

I went back to stabbing my food.

Once lunch was finished—or, in my case, abandoned—my mother wheeled me to my room. I had a roommate who spoke no English and shuffled across the floor to the bathroom at the speed of a sloth, leaning heavily on her walker. I was as mesmerized by her slowness as I was scared of it.

"If you close the curtain around your bed, it's like you're in your own private room," my mom said, in a sunny-side-up voice.

"I am not living with a curtain around me!"

I had requested a private room, but only two were up for grabs in my unit and both were taken. I should have felt grateful that I had a room at all—there was a long list of people waiting to get into Lyndhurst—but I was miserable and ready for a fight. A pink-scrubbed nurse with matching pink lipstick and white hair came to take my blood pressure and sift through my medical details. I tried to be friendly, but she seemed even less interested in me than I was in her.

"Well, she was a cold fish," my mother said when the nurse had left.

I tried to work up some anger to defend the cold fish, but settled instead for some wordless snarling.

My roommate began another slow shuffle around her bed and I clenched my fists to my mouth.

"Close the curtains, please," I ordered my mom, and she jumped out of her chair to do it. "All the way."

My mother read quietly beside me. I'd been horrible to her all day. It was best for both of us if she stayed close but also stayed quiet.

How was this going to work, I wondered? Although it felt like I had been at the hospital forever, it had been only nine days—just a short enough time to make the staff think I was (almost) always happy. But with those giddy morphine days behind me and an indefinite stay at Lyndhurst looming, there was no getting around the seriousness of my circumstances. I was already feeling responsible not only for my mood but for the mood of my nurses, my worried parents, my kids, Rich. Their good days would be dependent on *my* good days.

I searched my bag, found the three pictures that Henry had given me, and put them in my lap. There was one of Joey, looking away from the camera, hands on his hips in a superhero pose, a spectacular view of Machu Picchu behind him. There was also a picture of the four of us, sitting on a bench in a square in Cusco. I was wearing the jeans that had made my legs feel ravaged; you couldn't tell from the photo how uncomfortable I was. The last picture was of Rich and me, his arm around me, holding fast, as if I might fall back onto the ancient Inca steps behind us if he let go. We both look tired but happy. I found it hard to look at these photos.

Moments later, the doctor came to see me. She introduced herself then sat in a chair at the end of my bed. I pulled the covers a little more tightly around my legs. They were buzzing so crazily, they blocked out all other sensory perceptions. I couldn't even tell if I was wearing pants. She saw my pictures.

"You were in Peru," she said.

I nodded.

"My husband and I went," she said, "before we had kids."

"That's nice," I said. I didn't want to talk about Peru. I blamed

Peru for my current situation. Peru, with its leg-stealing Inca Trail. I hated Peru.

"Did you get altitude sickness?" she asked me.

"Yes," I told the doctor. "The altitude got to me."

"Did your husband get sick, too?"

I shook my head.

"Mine didn't, either. I'm in *way* better shape than him but I couldn't keep up. I brought a ton of pills in case this kind of thing happened to him, thinking it would *never* happen to me. But when it happened to me, I refused to take the pills."

I had also refused to take the altitude pills. But I didn't tell the doctor that.

"How do you feel?" she asked.

I didn't answer. "Coca tea! Coca tea!" I remembered the Peruvian cook call the morning after we had climbed for seven hours. I lay awake in my tent, searching wildly for my legs. My gloves snagged in my haste to rip the zipper off my sleeping bag. I shook my head to shake off the dream that had obviously broken through the gossamer screen between asleep and awake, but still, even as my eyes stared at my legs, my brain could not fathom where they were. I punched them, pounded my thighs hard enough to make my feet bounce off the ground until, it seemed, from memory alone, I was able to get them to stand up and walk out of the tent.

"Are you eating?" the doctor asked.

"I guess."

We ate quinoa porridge in Peru, so thin and milky it was more drink than food.

"Do you feel pain?" asked the doctor.

In Machu Picchu town, my rib cage had felt encased in a corset two sizes too small.

"Yes, I have pain," I told the doctor.

"On a scale of one to ten, how great would you say the pain is?"

"Let's just say six."

"Where do you feel the most pain?"

"My back."

"Trouble sleeping?"

I couldn't sleep at the hotel. They had mistakenly put us in twin beds. "Can't move my back, Rich. Can't move my back!" He woke up and gave me a Tylenol with codeine and told me to try to relax.

"I can sleep," I told the doctor.

"Trouble waking up?"

"No."

"So how are you feeling, generally speaking?"

I looked up, finally, at this petite, well-dressed woman in the chair at the end of my bed. Why, I wanted to ask her, did everyone always sit at the end of my bed several feet away from me? Even my own *feet* didn't want to be around me.

"Are you asking me if I'm depressed? Is that what all your questions are leading to?"

She smiled at me as if she had known me forever and knew how I "could get." I was not in the mood for being charmed or charming.

"What's your name again?" I had met so many doctors and nurses I stopped pretending to remember their names.

"Dr. Zimcik. The 'c' is silent. I totally should have changed my name."

"Dr. Zimcik, would *you* be depressed if you found out in the middle of your life that you couldn't walk?"

She smiled at me, and then just as quickly dropped the smile when she saw the look on my face. "Yes, I would."

"I'm not depressed," I said.

"Good."

"Were you going to suggest I take something?"

"Only if you thought you needed it."

"I don't."

She held up her hands. "Okay. Just checking."

"Sorry—what kind of doctor are you again?"

"I'm the GP here. I specialize in the general care of spinal cord patients."

"I see."

"I'll be checking in with you every day." She got up and stood right next to me. "You can ask me anything you want."

"Fine."

"I'll see you tomorrow, okay, Ruth?"

She squeezed my shoulder as she left and paused for a moment as if she wanted to say something more. Without knowing a thing about me, Dr. Zimcik made me feel like I was still the same person I was before. All she had to do was say my name.

6

Step 1—Learn How to Walk

I didn't know who my first visitor at Lyndhurst would be, but the last person I expected to see was one of Rich's clients, barely more than an acquaintance of mine. Aaron burst through my closed curtain carrying a giant vase of flowers that fully obscured his face. As I pulled my blanket up to my chest—taking note of the lax security situation—he plopped the vase on my windowsill and then leaned both his hands on the end of my bed like he was giving his calves a good stretch.

"Rich told me you weren't seeing any visitors, but I was in the neighborhood, so." He shrugged. "I came by."

As far as what visitors I would allow, it essentially came down to this: I would only see people I could fart in front of. From that perspective, the list was pretty long. But Aaron was not on this list. And because he was not, our visit quickly became exceedingly uncomfortable. As he talked, I writhed on the bed, my legs flopping this way and that, my fists occasionally pounding the mattress, trying to clench my bum, which was virtually impossible. Even with the tumor gone, I had to concentrate extra hard to figure out where my bum actually was.

"Aaron it's been really great to see you thanks for the flowers they're beautiful you have to go."

As soon as he left, I called Rich.

"I need a bodyguard."

"Oh, no. Who came?"

"Aaron."

"What?!"

"Yeah."

"I *just* got off the phone with him half an hour ago telling him *not* to visit."

"It didn't work, but I have some good news. I've been moved to a private room."

"You got a private room and Aaron saw it before me? That's just great."

Rich had worked so hard with my actors' union to secure me a private room in the (unlikely) event of a long hospital stay. If I raised my bed to a full sitting position, I could see perfectly out the south-facing window that looked onto a huge, dewy green lawn with a tantalizing glimpse of the ravine below. The grass was largely taken over by hyper dogs and their less-hyper owners. I have never been a dog person, but I made myself zero in on the movement of their quick furry legs as keenly as I studied the legs of their owners. My view would serve as an endless documentary on the mechanics of walking. It made me realize how much of my comic life, as both an actor and a civilian, had been tied up in the way I moved—with my hands and feet providing the bulk of my physical humor—but since my feet had gone rogue, try as I might, I could find nothing funny in their absence, so I looked out the window and took notes.

In those first few days at Lyndhurst, I was overwhelmed with visits from varying hospital staff. Dr. Zimcik, my new GP; Dr. Emm, the physiatrist who treated a variety of medical conditions affecting the spinal cord and nerves; the quiet, young resident chaplain; a social worker. They each had a very specific role to offer in my recovery if I chose to access their services. Because the only question I had for any of them was the only one I knew they couldn't answer, I barely said anything at all.

When will I walk again? Will I ever walk again? When will I walk again? Will I ever walk again? When? Will? When? Will? When?

I met my primary nurse, Rumy, on my second day there. I assumed I was not the first patient at Lyndhurst to take gait-studying to a whole new level, but I might have been the first one willing to trade in my old, very serviceable walk for a new one, and the walk I wanted was Rumy's. Her hips moved as if she were walking the shallow end of a pool—slow and languid—and she never rushed no matter how rushed she was. I wondered, if I learned to walk again, would my body naturally go back to the gait it had before or would the slate be wiped clean? I was concerned that the answer to that question was contained in my bum, which was now, as my son Joey so succinctly put it, a dumb-ass. My nervous system, from my belly button down to my baby toes, was firing madly but on different cylinders, my circuitry board having been rewired by a clown. I tried to picture my gait before all this happened, but I could only visualize myself in exaggerated moments: crouched low when my children were little, holding out my arms for them to come to me; affecting a model's walk when prancing around the house in a new pair of heels; sliding across the tile floor, in socks, surfer-style, to answer the front door. I told Rich how my greatest wish was to somehow unearth a video of me walking the way I did before all this happened.

Joey was the first to let me in on a little secret.

"Uh, Mom? Haven't you done like a few hundred episodes of TV? You think maybe you *walked* in any of them?"

Right! I could search YouTube, but it felt too soon. I wasn't ready to see myself as I once was.

On our first meeting, Rumy asked if I could transfer from my wheelchair to the bed by myself. Every time I was asked a question that began with "Can you," I felt a rush of petulance followed by a sour stream of anger. At St. Mike's it was the same thing: *Can you put your shoes on? Can you sit up? Can you tell me if your toes are moving up or down?* My first thought before I opened my mouth was always: *Are you people a bunch of fucking idiots?* Or worse: *Do you think* I'm *a fucking idiot?* I thought Rumy would be different. What person couldn't get from their chair to their bed without help? In the interest of starting off our relationship on the right foot, I swallowed my impulse to answer imperiously.

"I think so, yes," I said, with just the right amount of shyness and deference. *Now watch this.*

I held on tightly to the arms of my chair for leverage, then pulled my weight up, shifted over (so far, so good), then collapsed right in between the narrow space between my bed and the chair.

"Oh dear! Hold on!" Rumy said, then ran to get help.

While I clung to the space between the floor and the chair, using all the strength I could find, I thought of the neurologist Dr. Shure's fascination with my string-bean arms. When pressed into action, they proved stronger than the rest of my body put together. Rumy returned with another nurse and a four-foot-long wooden board to facilitate the transfer from my chair to the bed.

"I'm really sorry, Rumy," I said, once I was safely on the bed, staring at my knees like a chastened child.

"Don't worry about it," she said. "You'll figure out how to transfer in no time."

"I thought I could do it."

"And you will be able to soon enough."

"I keep forgetting why I'm here."

Of all the people I met when I first arrived, the only name I really cared about was the one on my weekly schedule pinned to my corkboard, the one person I had no choice but to meet with five times a week for the duration of my stay: Amanda, my physiotherapist.

I remembered that the punky, highly pierced girl Rich and I had met outside St. Mike's had told me her physiotherapist was Neil. She said there was another PT named Amanda, but that I should try to get Neil. I cursed my luck. The punky girl had told me how Neil made his patients walk up and down a steep hill in Sunnyside Park, behind the rehab clinic, as a condition of their discharge. I reveled in the image of me traipsing up a hill, my arms swinging, my legs steady and firm, sure of their place on the ground—Julie Andrews singing from the mountaintop, my whole face tipped toward the sky, triumphant.

My first few sessions with Amanda had an awkward feel to them, as if we were both trying to squeeze through a narrow doorway at the same time.

"I don't understand *how* to walk," I explained to her. "I can't remember what body parts I'm supposed to be activating or in what order. I don't know when to squeeze, when to lift, when to touch down. I don't *get* it." Then, I had an idea. "Amanda, would you mind walking across the room for me?"

Our bodies were very similar—both of us around five feet two, with the same smallish frame, but Amanda's body was packed more tightly than mine. Her walk had a refreshing, clean feel to it—like a blade of grass. I was certain that studying Amanda's gait would be easier than what I had been doing up to that point, which was watching YouTube videos of people walking around Manhattan, first at a normal pace and then in slow motion. I watched them over and over, pausing the video to take note of when a knee bent, where a foot landed, how the distance between the feet remained approximately the same after every step, how the walker looked around without veering off course. I was fascinated by each subject's almost arrogant entitlement to space and of how easily he or she fit inside it. I would cross check what I was watching on my computer against the dog walkers and toddler chasers outside my window. Between my sessions with Amanda and my YouTube homework, I resolved to cobble my old walk back together again.

But I continued to feel as if I had been cheated somehow. Based on that one brief conversation with the punky girl, I was convinced that Neil was the best possible choice for me. I saw him in the PT room. I watched him out of the corner of my eye, even as I tried to absorb what Amanda was telling me. Neil was wiry and quick. I could practically feel the heat of his energy burning off him. That's what I needed, I thought, someone who could whip me into shape in record time. Amanda's energy, by comparison, felt too slow, too measured, too safe. I thought I might never get out of Lyndhurst if I had to work at her pace. So I started lying to her in order to jump-start my recovery.

"Can you feel the floor today, Ruth?" Amanda asked. I was sitting on the blue plinth, staring at my feet. They were complete strangers to me.

"My feet feel quite floaty at the moment!" I said, neatly sidestepping her question, too afraid to tell her that, no, I couldn't feel the floor.

She was smiling at me, pleased—I think—that I could feel anything at all.

"That's great, Ruth. Let's get you up. I want you to hold on to my shoulders and I'll hold your thighs."

I watched as she gripped both of my legs with her small hands. "Can you feel that?"

"Sure!" I felt nothing.

"Great. Now I'm going to help you lift your right leg and place it on the plinth beside me so that you're standing on just your left leg. Don't worry, though—I've got you. Now, can you feel your left glute turn on?"

I squinted. "Wow! I think so!" My leg could have been wrapped around my head for all I knew.

Over the course of that first week, I realized something terrible: Amanda believed everything I said. Encouraged by my tone, which suggested my nerves were responding positively to all kinds of stimuli—touch, floor, fabric—she had an idea she thought might interest me.

"We're going to get you down on all fours," she said.

I felt a pressure in my chest, like I was being choked from the inside.

On a much wider plinth, one about the size of a queen-size bed, I got down on my hands and knees, swaddled on all sides by plastic-covered foam rectangles.

"So what's going to happen here?" I asked in my most raring-to-go voice.

The goal was simple enough: to remain in that position without tipping.

Meanwhile, across the way, Neil was bouncing around like a pogo stick while his patient alternated between smiling as if he was watching a circus act and frowning because he was the next performer up.

"I just want you to lift your right hand off the mat," Amanda said, carefully, so as not to frighten me. "Not too far, just a bit, and balance on your other hand and your knees. Can you try that?"

"Of course!" My heart beat wildly. *I can do this*, I thought. *The problem is not in my hands. I can feel my hands just fine, I can lift my hands, I've lifted my hands a million times before.* My knees were wobbling like mad. I stared at my hand, begging it to rise up, but my brain refused to let it happen. My hand was afraid to come up, knowing that the rest of my body could not balance without its support. *Come on*, I told it. *Just come up a little.* I smiled at Amanda. She was very still, watching me patiently, giving me the space I needed to figure it out on my own.

"Maybe," I said. "Maybe we can start with something else?"

"Sure, Ruth. No problem. How about you try lifting your left knee only. Not too high! Just a tiny bit off the mat."

"Good idea. I can do that." But I didn't know where my left knee was. I looked under my chest and toward my legs, but that made me dizzy. I started listing. The lump in my throat grew larger. I knew I could squeeze out only one more sentence so I wanted to make it worthwhile. "I want to go back in my chair!" I wailed, before falling over.

Amanda moved swiftly—the fastest I'd seen her move—to get me comfortably seated again. I wanted to be the best student she had ever seen—the best student *Neil* had ever seen, so that maybe he could poach me *away* from Amanda. I looked over at Neil. He was leaping up and down like a frog while his poor patient watched, utterly confused.

"This is all my fault," I said. "I don't know what I'm doing. I ask questions, but I don't understand the answers—or my body doesn't. I know you're trying, but I'm really confused. I need to take little sips, not giant gulps. I feel like I'm choking on information."

Amanda nervously played with her bangs while she tried to figure out how to respond. I could tell she was growing out her hair but was stuck in that middle stage where it was long enough to fall into her eyes but too short to tuck back behind her ears. She kept brushing her bangs aside anyway—her tiny act of futility somehow like my own.

"Amanda," I said, once the lump in my throat had safely retreated. "Here's what I think maybe we should do: just one thing at a time from now on, okay? I see now that it's the only way this walking thing is ever going to work out for me. If we work on one tiny thing at a time."

Amanda nodded her head, relieved. I suspected this was her plan all along before I decided to push my half-baked agenda on her. I looked at Neil and his patient again. He was bouncing on his toes. His patient looked like he had packed it in for the day.

"So that's okay with you?" I asked.

She nodded again. I didn't want her to think I was angry. I just needed to press the reset button. I smiled at her and she smiled back. We were now on the same team.

•

I thought that by the end of my first week at Lyndhurst, I had met all the staff members I was supposed to meet, but there was one more.

"Hello, Ruth! Can I come in?"

"Sure." A man's running shoes and wheels pulled up to my curtain as if my bedside were a parking spot.

He threw back the curtain with a *ta-da* flourish. He was younger than me, handsome, confident. I saw a folder on his lap, an official name in block letters across the top.

"I just wanted to introduce myself and tell you a little bit about the Canadian Paraplegic Association. I'll listen to your story and maybe I can tell you mine."

A silence followed while we sized each other up. His eyes darted over me like he was connecting the dots.

"You look really familiar to me," he said.

Perspiration bloomed above his eyebrows as if I had called it forth.

"I don't think so," I said. "What's your name?"

"Kellan."

Instinctively, I thought: *Be polite, don't encourage, find the nearest exit.*

I didn't think my story was any of Kellan's business and I resented his casual presumption that I had arrived at some sort of higher ground where I could look back with clarity on what had led me there. But there were steps I had to follow to get him to leave, so I did what was required of me, moving speedily from tingles to tumor to Lyndhurst. Then, sticking to my first rule—be polite—I asked with dread, "How did you get here?"

"Eighteen years ago, I started to have this recurring dream that a tree fell on me. I ignored it for as long as I could—after all, it was just a dream. But I found myself thinking about it too much during the day. It was affecting my school work, everything. So I told my mother, who reassured me that a dream is just a dream. My parents were building a cottage in a heavily forested area. We had a bunch of acres; it was going to be their dream retreat. My brother and I went up north with my dad to do some clear cutting. My dad and I hacked away at this one tree. The law of gravity dictates that when you cut it one way, it will fall the other way. I saw the tree falling toward me, but I wasn't fast enough, even with my father screaming at me to run."

The parts of my body that weren't buzzing were shivering.

"Anyway," Kellan said, "I'm paralyzed from the waist down."

That could have been me. I could have been paralyzed from the waist down.

In spite of my rule not to ask any questions, I asked: Exactly how many times did you have this dream? Had you ever cut down a tree before? Did the doctors ever lead you to believe that you'd walk again?

I, too, had had a premonition of something bad befalling me, but I wasn't about to admit that to Kellan. Before my very first appointment with Dr. Bright to discuss my tingly feet, I had become increasingly paranoid about two back-to-back raffles I had won. I didn't even care about the prizes; I had entered both raffles on a lark. The first win felt fluky, the second like an omen. They made me consider the other lotteries in my life, all of which I'd won—the guy lottery, kids lottery, friends lottery, career lottery. I had had to work hard to shake the feeling that something horrible was about to happen to me. The last thing I wanted was for Kellan to think he could recruit me to his Paraplegic Association just because I was in a hospital, lying down, with a wheelchair next to my bed. *I am not a fucking paraplegic!* I wanted to yell.

Instead, I blurted out, "Do you date?" Since the surgery I had been known to blurt out sexual non sequiturs.

"Sometimes."

"How does that happen?"

"What? How does that *work*?" His voice pitched upward and his face reddened.

"Wait, what? I didn't ask that! I meant how do you *meet* people?"

At St. Mike's one day, within seconds of my parents arriving for a visit, I had wailed, "Rich will never have sex with me again!"

"Of course he will," my bewildered father had said, a laugh falling out of his mouth in spite of his gross discomfort.

"He won't he won't he won't!"

My mother had jumped in, maybe to save me but probably more so to save my father.

"Honey," she said. "Nobody has ever loved someone as much as Rich loves you."

"It doesn't matter it doesn't matter! I'll never have sex again!"

"I would *never* ask a person that," I mumbled to Kellan. Now we were both staring at our laps, as if we were praying, or working through a really tough math problem.

Then Kellan clutched his agenda tightly in his hands. Using the embers of his embarrassment to stoke his cause, he told me with great fervor about the Canadian Paraplegic Association. As he talked about the benefits and hidden joys of his club, I had a bone-chilling thought: Did he know something about me that I didn't? Did he have access to my files? Was Dr. Ginsberg's French-press vote of confidence at the hospital merely a way of delaying the truth—that my wandering legs would never ground themselves, that I would never walk again?

"Kellan!" I said, cutting off his spiel. "I appreciate you coming in . . ."

Rule number one—be polite.

". . . but I don't want to know about your services. I've got enough on my mind. I have no room for this, *not one tiny scrap of room, Kellan.*"

"I hear ya, Ruth. I understand. But would you be interested in membership?"

"Membership? Membership in *what*?"

He held up his folder like it was exhibit A. "The CPA."

"No."

"Can I ask you a few questions from my questionnaire?"

"Fine."

He placed the folder on his still legs as if his lap was his de facto desk.

"Your date of birth."

"Pardon?"

"When were you born?"

"June 7, 1965. Why?"

"Your address."

"Excuse me?"

"Your address," he said, evenly.

"Why on earth do you need my address, *Kellan*?"

"So we can send you material when you make the transition home in your wheelchair."

I felt sick thinking of the words *home* and *wheelchair* in the same sentence. "No! Enough!" I turned away from him and looked out the window, where my people walked and laughed and chased dogs. "I'm not answering any more of your questions."

He put the package on my bed and I swung back on him. "And by the way, I'm on TV, okay? *That's* why I look familiar to you. I would normally say, oh, maybe we went to high school together, maybe we met in line at Costco, maybe we this maybe we that, but let's face it—none of those things happened. You were watching TV and you flicked past my face scolding Billy Ray Cyrus or or or being some kid's mother on some kid's TV show and that's where you saw me, okay? We don't know each other."

I turned back toward the window and instantly felt like an idiot. Maybe he *had* seen me at Costco. The second I heard the curtain *whoosh* closed, I flung Kellan's folder onto my windowsill where the CPA logo landed faceup.

That night, I couldn't sleep. The following day, a new nurse tended to me. Young and super eager, her hands shook as she tried to attach the IC to empty my bladder. While she poked around looking for the right hole ("This has never happened to me before! I'm so sorry!"), she told me a feel-good story about a quadriplegic who had walked out of Lyndhurst.

"If he was a quad," I asked, "what would I be considered?"

"Do you really want to know?"

I said nothing.

"An incomplete paraplegic."

I looked steadily at her, preparing to fight her on this ridiculous assessment, but she was smiling at me with such unreserved brightness, I wondered if maybe she was a bit off.

"I have to tell you something," she said, unable to hold it in any longer. "I'm a huge *Degrassi* fan!"

And then, perhaps to emphasize her point, she rolled me over and shoved a "magic bullet" up my bum.

•

"Touches." In my previous life as an actress, "touches" were what you had right after lunch, and before you started shooting again—a quick go-over in the hair and makeup chair to ensure that you were camera-ready. But in this new context, "touches" meant a nurse squatting next to you while you sat on the commode, her face level with your thighs while you read, or tried to read, or played with your phone or wrote lists or otherwise made busywork to distract from the latex-gloved finger wrapped in the blue plastic square, like a finger ice cream cone, twisting up your bum to fish out a poo. It was a well-known fact (although I didn't know this until months later, having stubbornly avoided all Internet searches regarding this subject) that for those with SCIs, walking is only slightly less difficult than regaining bladder and bowel function. My physiotherapy was rarely scheduled before eleven A.M. because "touches" sometimes required a full morning's labor to produce results, if any. It was also why I forbade anyone from visiting before noon. Morning, I would tell people with a forcefulness no one dared question, was not the best time.

My rehab bathroom was three times bigger than my own doll-size one at home, and tricked out for even the most disabled resident's use. Once "touches" were over, I would remain on the commode and then roll up next to the bathtub without actually getting into it. The bathroom floor sloped gently toward the center of the room so the water could run toward the drain. There were hand railings on all walls, a harness hanging from the ceiling over the toilet for patients who needed to be lowered onto it, emergency pull cords reachable from any place one might slip, a shelf beside the toilet that housed not just toilet paper but also the ubiquitous beige latex gloves and oversized squares of blue plastic.

Showering consisted of me sitting naked while Rumy washed my back, calves, and feet with the handheld showerhead, then passed it to me so I could wash all the body parts I was able to access on my own. I didn't even try to pull in my stomach or sit up taller to make my breasts look less swingy—I couldn't be bothered. Rumy would poke tiny holes in the silence with gentle chatter.

"My son got a job at the grocery store."

"Uh-huh."

"Sobeys."

"Ah. Which one?"

"Off Marlee."

"Oh. I know that one." In fact, Rich had developed a new routine since I'd been gone. He would take Henry to that grocery store a few nights a week to buy the boys all the things that I wouldn't: sugary cereals, bacon, ham, Asian pears, Oreos.

"Henry loves that store," Rich told me. "I love it, too."

"I'm really glad," I said, and I was, but it also made me miserable. Did anybody in my house miss me as much as I missed them?

Rumy wasn't the kind to affect false cheer or to buoy me up with overly large smiles and useless platitudes. She gave me unspoken permission to be my miserable self when I wanted to. But the shower was an elixir. My feet, despite their lack of understanding in the up/down department, could still feel the difference between hot and cold, a lucky break that was rare among SCIs. The heat and the rush of water awakened all my joyous cells, cells that lay dormant until activated by very specific stimuli. They couldn't always be accessed by visitors or by my kids or by unexpected gifts delivered to my room in elaborately bowed boxes, but the *whoosh* of water against my skin never failed to make me feel happy to be alive.

One morning, my occupational therapist, Heidi, made a rare trip to my room.

"Looks like Amanda is going to be away today," she told me. "So I thought we could do something in the OT room instead. Sound good?"

"Fine. You might want to sit down." I was in the middle of a battle with my shoes. "This could take a while."

I always wore shoes to physio, although never during physio. I could barely reach over, reach down, grab the shoelaces, and then, once I had finally gotten my drunken left foot down and into the mouth of my shoe, I simply had to go on faith that it had hit bottom. The whole futile exercise frustrated me to the point of tears, but I had made the decision, many days earlier, not to cry in public anymore. Instead, I more or less panted like a porn star.

"There!" I said. My floaty feet were in and my laces tied. Heidi nodded her head slowly, impressed.

In the OT room, I transferred onto the plinth while she rigged some MacGyver-type contraption to help get me back on my feet. I thought occupational therapy was just for figuring out how to access your stove from a sitting position, or for introducing one to the wonders of long-handled back scrubbers, but not today. There was a pointer, a felt pen, a huge whiteboard, the plinth, and a chair. I felt like a contestant on a new game show: Wheelie of Fortune. While Heidi and her assistant set things up, I sat quietly. I rocked back and forth a little, stopped, rocked back and forth again, stopped. I thought: *There's something stuck on the back of my pants.* It wasn't painful or overly uncomfortable, but I wasn't sure I liked it. I shifted, but the thing attached to my bottom shifted with me. I was growing increasingly aggravated. I slid my hand under my right butt cheek, but turned up nothing.

After watching me grope for a while, Heidi asked, "What's going on?"

"I think there's a pen in my pants," I said. It felt long, narrow, kind of hard.

"I think it's your bum," she said.

"But it's *under* my bum."

"No, I think it *is* your bum. I think you just found your sit bone."

She waited.

"I think your right butt cheek just turned on," she said, spelling it out for me.

My right butt cheek was back! It felt weird, it felt foreign, but it was back. I rocked one way, then the other, giving my bum a hug from above. One butt cheek down, one more to go.

•

Each morning, I called home and spoke to Rich and the kids, got up to speed on the shape of their days, got off the phone and cried, endured my "touches," and—depending on the results— cried again. After that, I would wheel around my room loading up my purse with supplies to ensure I wouldn't have to look at any of the other patients: two pairs of sunglasses, a notebook and pen, a pencil for my *Globe and Mail* crossword puzzle, and an entertainment magazine. Packing my purse was easy; parking it on my lap, not. I would wheel a few feet and the purse would slide off. I would bend down (carefully, carefully), swipe it off the floor, then slap it back on my lap, then wheel a few more feet before it would slide off again. I would do the same thing over and over but expect a different result until I noticed one day that the strap on my purse was long enough to wind around the handlebars at the back of my chair. So that's what I did, twisting painfully behind me to the right, then to the left, to sling my purse over the curved rubber knobs. But the strap was too long and the wheels of my chair rubbed up against the leather, which both slowed me down and gave my bag wheel burn. I unslung the bag from the handlebars and slammed it back down on my lap, then held it in place with one hand while I wheeled forward with the other, switching hands every few feet to steer so that I didn't end up spinning in half-baked circles like a dog chasing a squirrel. It was five weeks before I had my lightbulb moment: I needed a knapsack.

After enlisting Rich to purchase one for me, I realized I had another problem: My hands had become raw and blistered from pushing the wheels of my chair. A very good-looking staff member, who also happened to be a paraplegic, found me in front of the elevator one morning rubbing my hands. He had a suggestion.

"Get the leather gloves with the little balls on them. They have maximum grip." He held out his gloved hands for me to see.

I was reluctant to ask Rich to find some for me—buying them felt like cementing my fate. I asked him what he thought a good alternative might be.

"What about Henry's batting gloves?"

"But he's going to need them."

"I'll talk to him."

"Here, Mom," Henry said on his next visit. "Try these."

"Are you sure, honey?"

"Yep."

They were his tiny white batting gloves with the snap enclosure around the wrist. They fit me perfectly. I wore them every day after that, and the blisters disappeared.

7

Step 2—Learn How to Have Sex Again

Time acquired elastic properties at Lyndhurst, collapsing, then stretching to unimaginable lengths. I didn't know whether to be surprised at how quickly my new wheelchair had been made for me or aggravated at how long it took. While I counted every-thing—minutes in the bathroom, hours until lunch, seconds until the end of physio—the days themselves seemed to quickly vanish so that I wasn't sure whether my chair had taken a lifetime to make or was made in record time.

Either way, when Heidi wheeled it into my room, eight or nine days into my stay, my first thought was, *It's so cute!* Heidi and I assessed its merits like it was a new car. I wasn't sure what was expected of me. *Do I take it for a spin? Kick the tires? Inhale that new wheelchair smell?* Upon closer inspection, it didn't seem quite right.

"Why is it *so* tiny?" I asked.

"Well, I guess you're not exactly a giant."

She helped me into it. It felt like a pretty good fit even if my body couldn't be trusted to get anything right. The chair was also easily collapsible, which paved the way to an unanticipated perk:

Rich and I could leave the hospital to celebrate our sixteenth anniversary. It would be my first time off Lyndhurst grounds.

In preparation for our big night out, we met Heidi in the parking lot one afternoon to practice transferring me from my chair into the car and from the car back into the chair. Rich learned how to dismantle the chair, fit it into the trunk, reassemble it, and transfer me back into it. The whole process was oddly exhilarating and after two or three perfect transitions, we declared ourselves date-ready.

Saturday night was quiet at Lyndhurst. I didn't spot any of the regulars while I waited in the lobby for Rich. A burly security guard I didn't recognize sat at the receptionist post. We nodded at each other like we were both there on official business. I nervously slid my hands along the arms of my new chair. While I waited, I had time to contemplate the key to happiness. Could it be as simple as always having something to look forward to? The Holy Grail for me, at that time, was threefold: to walk; to get my bodily functions back; and to get my sexual function zipping along. But while I tried to figure out how to achieve all those things, there were literally dozens of precious small moments that helped my spirits remain buoyant. Daily showers; visitors for lunch; lunch; Rich; my boys; *The Globe and Mail* crossword; turning over in bed by myself; tying my shoes; eating apples after physio; sitting in the sun; Dr. Zimcik; jujubes.

But actually leaving the hospital to celebrate our anniversary presented the kind of wish fulfillment I hadn't dared entertain. I don't remember who voiced the idea or how it gained traction. But no one tried to stop me—not the security guard who couldn't have been blind to the amount of makeup I was wearing—and certainly not my nurses, who seemed as invested in my date as they were in what might happen after.

My French rock 'n' roll nurse, Juliette, was adamant I wear my green silk shirt instead of the see-through one I had chosen.

"It's your arms," she said, rubbing her own arms. "You must show your arms. Plus the green—*c'est très très bon.*"

"But with my see-through number you can see everything—*including* my arms," I argued. "I'm sticking with the see-through."

She popped in and out of my room several times during the day of my date with more and more hints as to how I should *end* the evening. There was no doubt in my mind that Juliette had the best sex life of any nurse I had ever met. She told me to enlist my friends to buy me electric candles.

"Place them on the windowsill to avoid having to turn on the fluorescent lights." She wrinkled her little French nose to register her distaste at the lack of romantic lighting in my room. "As long as your curtain and door are shut, no one will come in." She went so far as to remind me that I should pee after to make sure I didn't get a bladder infection, completely forgetting that I couldn't actually pee on my own.

Rumy took a more practical approach to my date, reminding me that I had to get my nerve medication before I left and to make sure I had enough painkillers to get me through the evening. Sonja, my Russian nurse/handmaid, could do little more than hold her hands together under her chin and beam at me like I was her only daughter going to the prom.

I refused to wear leggings for our night out. I somehow managed, without any assistance, to wriggle into my skinny jeans while ignoring the noisy protest that broke out the second my calves caught wind of my plan. I suppose I could have just worn a dress since the weather was still fine, but the last thing I wanted was to put my legs in an even more vulnerable state by leaving them exposed. Plus, as evil as my jeans were, the feeling in my legs was only magnified when my bare thighs touched each other. Since there was ultimately nothing I could wear that would be comfortable, I picked my outfit purely for its sex appeal. As I pulled my top on, it occurred to me that the only parts of my body that registered normal sensation anymore were my arms and my head.

I wore my black ballet flats even though there was no possible way they would stay on my feet—my toes had no grip and virtually no feeling. I found some red lipstick—a color I rarely wore—in my makeup bag and applied that carefully but mightily, along with a liberal amount of eyeliner, which I painstakingly drew right along my water line like a slutty teen. I used whatever cosmetic weapons I had in my arsenal to direct Rich's gaze away from my chair and back to my erstwhile desirability.

As I waited in the lobby, the oxycodone began to wear off. I could feel the first fiery spikes of pain beginning their ascent, two steel rods shoved up my back. I leaned forward, but there was no relief. I crossed my legs and with that one movement, I was able to distract myself from the tug-of-war in my back. This latest addition to my sitting style was courtesy of a particularly enigmatic patient at Lyndhurst. She was very attractive in a stripper kind of way, probably the fittest patient there. Mostly, she hung around the lobby wearing tight velour sweat suits and hanging with her good-looking, tough-guy boyfriend. She looked like she owned the joint but hated everyone who worked for her. I liked to imagine that the second she got her walking papers she would trash her room like a rock star and then leave with her middle finger held high in the air—*fuck you, wheelies!* When I first saw her, I quickly figured out why I found her so captivating: She crossed her legs.

It hadn't occurred to me that this was possible, but once I tried it, I never looked back; no more sad-looking splayed legs for me. The only time that kind of lax posture was acceptable was when I was deep into my pregnancies and I needed my legs to hold up my belly, which was holding up my bowl of chips. It took me a few tries to get the up, over, and around thing, but before long I was crossing my legs like a champ.

I wondered if I had remembered to tell Rich about the latest development with my back. Just a couple of days earlier, Rumy had taken out half the staples from the incision where the tumor had been removed.

"Do you want to lie down while I do it?" she had asked, holding the staple remover in the palm of her hand. It was exactly the same kind of staple remover one uses to remove staples from paper. There was nothing medical looking about it, because it was a *staple remover.*

I was naked at the time, sitting on my commode after having taken my shower, a small towel draped across my legs.

"Just do it here." I gripped the arms of the commode.

"A distraction, maybe?" she asked.

"Phone, please."

I sent texts while she pulled out thirteen of the twenty-seven staples that ran in a track down my back. I made her count them out loud as she plucked them, and then count them again after I heard their metallic *plink* on the plastic tray.

"I feel really stressed out," I said once she was done, and then started my porno pant. "Why can't we just do the rest of them now? I don't want to have to do this again." I was crying and whining and I hated myself for both.

"It's just the way it's done," Rumy said, placing a calming hand on my shoulder. "Some now, the rest later."

"Does everyone cry here?" I asked.

Rumy thought about this. She always made me feel as if I were her only patient, which meant that sometimes I acted as if I was.

"Yes," she said. "Everyone here cries."

•

Rich pulled up in front of the glass doors. I tried to sit up a little straighter in spite of the pain I felt when I moved too quickly.

There would be no crying tonight. I watched as he got out of the car and did a little jog around the back of it. The doors parted automatically and we beamed at each other as he walked toward me. He was wearing my favorite jeans—not his favorites—the ones he thought were too tight but I loved them. He had on his indigo shirt—also my favorite—and a dark blue blazer. His head was freshly shaved, bald and shiny as new. I could picture him looking in the mirror, wanting to be perfect. He bent down to kiss me and then kept his face close to mine.

"I'm nervous," he whispered.

"Me, too."

As he wheeled me out, the security guard gave us the thumbs up and we gave him the thumbs up back.

We managed the transfer into the car, but it wasn't easy. My back was in full-on revolt. The steel rods were stealing their way up my rib cage. They would not stop their ascent until they hit my scapula. An oxy would have taken care of the pain, but I had to wait until after dinner when I was safely back at Lyndhurst. In the meantime, I decided, a vodka martini would do just fine. Once in the passenger seat, I smoothed down the front of my jeans and touched the silvery bling around my V-neck. Rich got in the car.

"All good?" he asked.

"*So* good."

We found a parking spot right outside the restaurant, Mogette, on an otherwise packed street but felt our luck dry up as we stared at the sidewalk.

"We forgot about the curb," I said, when he came to open the car door for me.

"Should we go back?" he asked.

"Are you crazy?"

"What can I do?"

"Have you got the brakes on?"

Rich pushed the chair as close as he could to the edge of the curb and locked the brakes. "Should I lift you?" he asked.

I shook my head, then I put my hand up and grabbed the left arm of the chair with my right hand and without any further thought, pulled myself up out of the passenger seat and pretty much tossed myself into the chair like I was both discus and thrower.

Relief and excitement flooded through me. "Yes!" I said. "Did it!"

"Jesus Christ," said Rich.

He rolled me to the front door. I stared at it for a couple of seconds. Was the doorway wide enough to accommodate the chair? But my husband had done his research. He had spoken to the owner in advance to make sure every part of the restaurant was wheelchair accessible. Two men in long flapping half aprons rushed to meet us. One stood at attention while the other pulled the door wide-open and welcomed us in like we were the sole reason the restaurant was open so early.

"Hello, hello!" they both said. I felt like a celebrity, or a dowager, as they saw us to our table. A quick-thinking waiter removed the chair from my side—it wouldn't be needed. The restaurant was almost full even though it was barely six. Some diners were looking at me; I was certain I wasn't just imagining it. I smiled brightly, not just because I was genuinely happy to be there, but because I was hoping to project onto these strangers the impermanence of my situation. I hoped they could see that, although bound to a wheelchair, I carried myself like a woman who had been around the block a few times; like a woman who had *walked* around the block a few times. I badly wanted to telegraph every great moment of my past onto these diners so that they could feel free to stop looking at me with pity. *It's a lovely Saturday night*—my smile said—*and we're all here to have a nice meal and hey, since you're looking anyway, please note my crossed legs—it's entirely possible a stripper taught me this trick.* Which was when I looked down and saw that not only had my legs become uncrossed but one foot was missing a shoe.

"Oh, crap," I said. "Honey, can you please find my shoe and while you're down there, have a quick look around for my left foot? I think it might be under the footrest." It was the first of many times that night when Rich would disappear under the table and reappear with my shoe.

We ordered too much, laughed loudly, shook our heads in wonderment at the way things had turned out. I also drank too much and I cried after all. The waitstaff was as attentive as if it had been my birthday or my last supper, which made me wonder if they thought I might be dying. The owner brought us cake without us having ordered it. HAPPY ANNIVERSARY was written on the plate in something tart and delicious. As I licked the last bit of icing off my fork, I thought: *This is the best anniversary we have ever had.*

After dinner we left the restaurant and turned left. We passed the secondhand clothing store I used to walk by every day with Joey in his stroller; then the dry cleaner's where the owner and I mostly chatted about our kids before he returned my jeans to me, always shortened too short; then the corner store where Joey and I would get Popsicles when I was pregnant with Henry. If we had turned left again, we would have found ourselves right in front of our old house. I asked Rich to stop. A longing for my old life scrabbled to the surface, knocking aside everything in its path, including my happiness.

"I'm ready to go back now," I said.

Perhaps to Nurse Juliette's disappointment, I hadn't asked anyone to buy me electric candles. Rich wheeled me back to my room and kissed me good-bye before heading home. As sad as I was to see him leave, I needed desperately to tend to my back, which had erupted into flames. I was so late with my pain medication,

I would be playing catchup all night. Every part of my body was crying out for some kind of relief; I didn't know where to start first. I pushed the button on my bed to lower it so it was level with my chair, then, wincing so hard I pushed tears out of my eyes without actually crying, I transferred onto my bed. I didn't even bother changing out of my clothes first. I lay on my side until a nurse came with my oxycodone.

Our "after" would have to come later.

•

In many ways, it was just another lazy Saturday: coffee and paper in the morning, late shower, talking on the phone with my girlfriend. Only, I woke up alone and crying, counting down the hours until Rich arrived with the kids. I had been tipped off the day before that there would be a good lunch in the dining room.

"Make sure the boys arrive hungry, okay, Rich?"

Neville, my daily apple supplier, furtively gave Joey and Henry mac and cheese.

"I didn't give you nuthin' and you don't owe me nuthin'," he said, before tossing an extra dollop on each of the boys' plates. I loved Neville.

After lunch, we went outside. Rich wheeled me as far as the smoker's gazebo before Henry insisted on taking over, pushing me fast enough to blow my hair back. Rich yelled at him to slow down. Joey hung back, staring into his cell phone. The closer the time came for them to go home, the more anxious I became, until I just wanted them all to leave. What had been a genuine, happy smile plastered on my face all afternoon had morphed into a mask I couldn't wait to tear off. I needed to be alone with my buzzing legs that also felt like bulging sausages squeezed by too-tight elastic bands. I was desperate for my breakthrough medication even though I knew I would pay for it with a particularly difficult "touches" session the next day. My back throbbed. I insisted we say our good-byes from my room instead of the lobby. I couldn't bear the thought of watching my family as they walked to the car and drove home without me. Also, I had learned something crucial about myself since landing in the hospital: I needed to fall apart a little bit every day. Morning cries took care of that quite nicely, but on the days when the boys visited, crying just the one time didn't cut it. Sensing the change in my mood, Rich hastily got my pajamas ready and laid out my clothes for the following day. He hugged and kissed me, then made way for the boys. Henry collapsed in a heap on my lap, whispering good-bye a thousand times and then waving to me all the way to the elevator. Joey let himself be hugged but refused to move his arms from his sides.

I was alone again, the day gone as if it had never happened.

I thought about Joey more than I thought about Henry, even though Henry is younger. I saw how he wanted to be around me but didn't want to get too close. I saw how he never looked at my legs or at my eyes, which meant he was always in search of a safe spot to rest his gaze: the wall behind my head, his phone, my shoulders. But when I texted him, he would respond in seconds and sometimes he wrote, "How is your walking today?" Whenever I said, "I love you," which was every day, he would say, "K, bye," which I decoded to mean, "I love you, too."

But he was more observant than I realized. Rich called me after one of our weekend visits.

"Joey suggested I bring you your coffeemaker."

"*Joey* did?"

"He knows you miss coffee."

"Do you think he misses me?"

"I know he does."

Rich brought me the coffeemaker, but to use it, I needed Rumy's help. Her skills, while multifold, didn't extend to coffee-making.

She swore a lot and I could see for the first time that she was starting to lose her cool.

"Rumy, it's okay," I said. "Just pass it over here."

She put the Cuisinart clunker on top of my tray-on-wheels. I scooped my ground coffee into the paper filter and poured in the water. Rumy pressed a few buttons and then we both watched as the machine magically transformed the grounds into my favorite drink in the world. All the sounds—the gurgling, the dripping, the low rumble—were the sounds of home. Rumy brought me a Styrofoam cup and some milk from the kitchenette, then left. I made my coffee exactly the color I liked, exactly the way I liked, but I put my cup down after just a couple of sips. It went cold on my tray.

A few minutes later, Rumy popped her head around the curtain, smiling and expectant. "How was it?"

"Perfect," I said.

"Right on!"

Then I dutifully spread my legs for her to do my IC.

"Rumy," I said. "Will I ever have sex again?"

"Of *course* you will. We have *quad*riplegics who have sex again. There's no reason why you can't have sex. None."

This happened all the time. I would swerve off topic and Rumy would swerve with me.

"But will I feel anything?"

I closed my eyes. I couldn't tell when the catheter went in or when it came out. "I'll be honest with you," I said, knowing that being a patient at Lyndhurst was like living inside a truth factory. "I used to be a pretty orgasmic girl. I'm not prepared to say goodbye to all that."

"I don't think you have to," she said. "It'll just be more . . ." She looked up at the ceiling as if the word she was looking for were written there. "Psychological."

Her careful phrasing plunged me to a new low. I knew the brain was the sexiest organ of the body, but the workload on my brain was heavy enough as it was. While I spent an inordinate, almost inconceivable, amount of time each day thinking about sex, none of those thoughts were remotely sexy. I was consumed with the most rudimentary mechanics of things, like a sixteen-year-old pondering the eventual loss of her virginity. *Would it hurt? Would my nerves freak out? Would it feel the same? Would I feel anything at all?* Meanwhile, the daily facts of my reality pretty much killed the indulgence in all things erotic. Every day, I got a paper cup full of pills. On alternate days I was given three milk of magnesia tablets, two laxatives, and a stool softener. I took two vitamin Ds because not spending sufficient time outdoors meant that I required sunshine in a pill; two Tylenol Extra Strength to get me over the hump between oxy doses; and six gabapentin for my nerves, although it was originally formulated to treat epilepsy, which confused me.

"As I understand it," Dr. Zimcik explained, "and from what other patients have told me, the gabapentin turns down the noise in your body."

So I wasn't the first patient to register nerve confusion as noise.

No one could give me a straight answer as to what I could expect from my actual nerve recovery; it was impossible to pin down their erratic nature. Nerves fell into a completely separate category from muscle or bone, both of which followed a rigorous healing process that almost always guaranteed success. If muscle and bone are rule-followers, nerves are complete shit-disturbers. My body was in a constant state of surprise. Anything that touched my feet, for example, triggered a dramatic response so out of proportion to the alleged crime that I wanted to yell: *They're JUST SOCKS!* It was almost unbearable to lie on my side, even though this was the best position for my back, because when my naked thighs touched each other, it was as if Woody Allen and Mia Farrow were being forced to hug. But while my thighs were enemies, my feet were Romeo and Juliet. No matter how much I tried to keep them apart, invariably they ended up snuggling, sometimes strangling each other in the sheets. And when my bum wasn't feeling as if it had been exposed to a hot plate, it would go completely numb, so numb I would have to look down to make sure I was still wearing pants. I learned that nerves, while masters at rattling, were equally adept at playing dead. And it made me wonder: What else in me was dead?

There were so many concerns vying for first position on my list of priorities I sometimes didn't know where to start, but every day I knew where to end—with a Google search. *Sex and spinal cord injuries. Orgasms and spinal cord injuries. Woman's sex life after spinal cord surgery.*

In my searches, I found a plethora of pages fueled by panicked women wondering what would become of their sex lives once spinal shock settled into spinal calm. I skimmed the words, zeroing in on the ones I thought offered the most hope, only to be disappointed over and over. Certain that they couldn't all be pointing in the same disheartening direction, I would keep scrolling through the search engine until, one night, I landed on a YouTube video of a nurse practitioner named Dianne who had made a series of two-minute videos aimed at, well, me.

Dianne smiled warmly while she said there was no reason why I couldn't have sex. This was a good start. Given the overwhelming number of articles on erectile dysfunction in men with SCIs, I counted myself lucky just to be a woman. But it was one thing to be able to do it, another entirely to *feel* it. Dianne continued to smile warmly as she told me that whatever sensation had been lost post-surgery from the site of injury on down would not return. My injury was at the T5 level. I had discussed this with Dr. Zimcik. I knew that T5 fit squarely in between my shoulder blades, but

I wasn't sure if it corresponded exactly with a spot on the front of my body.

"Right at the nipple," Dr. Zimcik told me, holding her hands up in front of her breasts like they were being served on a tray. From my nipples down meant that fully three quarters of my body was sensitivity impaired.

"Oh," I said. "That explains a lot."

It explained why I would sometimes forget to take off my bra before I went to bed—my breasts, previously a huge issue in every way, were rendered a nonissue overnight.

"But the sensations *will* come back, right?"

"I don't think *that* will, but—" She was quick to jump on top of her own sentence when she saw me starting to sputter. "Other things will, Ruth. Other things *will* come back."

"I'll never have an orgasm again!"

"I feel strongly that you will."

"You don't know. *Nobody* knows!"

"I've seen the numbers from your IC. You need the IC less and less and are able to pee on your own more and more. This is a *very* good sign."

I just kept shaking my head, but Dr. Zimcik could tell I was listening, so she kept going.

"The nerves that control your bladder are very close to the nerves that control your sexual responses. Do you understand what I'm saying?"

I shook my head.

"I feel very confident that once you've mastered one, you will master the other."

I kept shaking my head.

"You have to give yourself a break, Ruth. Just give it time."

I was done with giving things time, done with ceding control to the state of my nerves. Nerves were more than just a control panel on my spine; they were my chutzpah, and the time to exercise it was right now. Rich was going to Joey's high school curriculum night the next day. I waited until I was pretty sure it was over and then I called him in the car.

"Hey, babe. Can you pop by here for a few minutes?" I asked.

"Sure."

I waited for him to walk into the room before I made the bed go all the way down, then I switched off the lights.

"What's going on?" he asked, knowing exactly what was going on.

"Come here."

"There's not enough room on that little bed for me."

"I think there is."

"Okay, Ru."

He lay down beside me. We kissed for a long time, as if we were new to this, as if there was no possibility of going any further so we might as well make the most of it. He rubbed my back and I felt a little bit here, nothing over there, and then a little bit somewhere else. I thought he touched my bum, but I was wearing pajama bottoms and I couldn't really tell.

"Go under my pants," I said. "Ah, I can feel that."

I felt like a teen in my parent's house, making out in the living room while my mom and dad watched *Barney Miller* upstairs.

"Take off your pants," I whispered.

"Ru . . . ?"

"Take off your underwear, too."

I took off my pants and underwear, neither of which was easy to do or sexy to watch, I'm sure. Rich did the same and when he did, all his credit cards slid out of his wallet and onto the floor. He got back into bed without even looking at them and we pressed against each other. He smelled the same as always—an intoxicating mix of green jujubes and Diet Coke—and I kept inhaling him, hoping his smell might trigger something deeper in me. I pressed him against me so hard. I could feel him, but it was taking forever to trigger a response in my body. It was as if all my nerves had nodded off when what I actually wanted was for the noisier ones to shut up, not the whole damn system to shut down completely. I chose not to think about it. Through pure instinct, my spaced-out legs hooked over his legs and then his hips. They had done this move thousands of times; they knew where to go. I was proud of them. I had no idea where my feet were, however, until I felt them bang into each other and then pull apart, a little surprised at the force of their collision.

"Let's do it," I said.

"Really?"

"Yeah, let's do it."

"But someone could come in."

"Rumy's the only one around. The door is shut, the curtain is closed, she won't come in." I moved the call bell so I wouldn't roll into it.

"Are you sure?"

"Rumy told me I could have sex."

"I don't want to hurt you."

"You won't hurt me."

I concentrated hard on what Rich was doing. I put mental checkmarks into little boxes: *felt that, felt that, not sure what's going on there, ah—felt that*. It wasn't the same as before surgery, but then again, nothing was.

"Well, we did it," I said after.

"That was crazy. Are we even allowed to do that in here?"

"Don't know, don't care."

"I don't care, either." He kissed me on the forehead, then got out of bed, pulled on his jeans, and started picking up all his credit cards.

"It will be different now," I warned.

"I know."

"And I mean, why shouldn't it be, right? How can things *not* change after a major life event like this? It's silly—it's *naïve* to think it won't. I mean, look at us."

We looked around my room. My windowsill held one vase of dead flowers and one vase of almost-dead flowers, plus five vases with no flowers and a long-handled shower brush that I never used. There were the three framed pictures of us from our trip to Machu Picchu taken in July, only two months earlier, and which I still found difficult to look at. There was a binder with MARSHALL on the side welcoming me to Lyndhurst, which I'd stopped reading after the first page. There was IC paraphernalia everywhere—catheters, blue felt squares, latex gloves, individually wrapped wipes—apples that I'd begun hoarding, Styrofoam cups, and a plastic pitcher that all patients had delivered to their room each morning along with their breakfast. The pitcher had a straw in it. I hated that. Who uses a straw to drink directly from a pitcher? Didn't people just pour out what they needed into cups? And then I remembered that although my legs didn't work, other people's hands didn't work, or their necks couldn't bend, or, like young Jimmy next door to me, they were blind.

We were sitting on the edge of my bed. Rich was dressed and ready to go but not ready to go. We smiled at each other. *Bet nobody else in this joint just did that*, said the thought bubble between our heads.

"You should know something," I said.

"What's that?"

"I'm telling Rumy."

"Oh no no no you're not."

"I have to. She's my nurse. I tell her everything."

"Oh God." But he couldn't deny me. Rich has never denied me anything. "Then I'm gonna split before she gets back."

"Okay, babe," I said. "I's loves ya."

"Me, too." Rich left, and I went to the bathroom and tried to pee. I couldn't wait for Rumy to come back. I couldn't wait to tell her. I also couldn't wait to stand up and stroll over to the nurse's station with my bags in my hands and say, "Ladies, you've been awesome, and I hope I never see any of you again." Having sex made me even more impatient. *Obviously*, went my thinking, *only walking people have sex. Ergo, I could walk.* The race was on between joy over having had sex and a complete breakdown over not being able to pee. I gave up on peeing and wheeled myself over to the sink. Just then, Rumy came in. I watched her reflection in the mirror behind me. I could tell from the look on her face that she already knew.

"I had sex!"

"Right *on!*"

That night, I went to sleep so happy. The next morning, I woke up with a bladder infection.

8

Step 3—Standing Up for Myself

One morning, I opened my eyes to an epiphany so obvious I felt like an idiot for having taken so long to recognize it: I was homesick. I started crying. I waited for Rumy to arrive, but when I remembered it was her day off, I cried even more. I called Rich knowing he wouldn't be able to talk to me—he would be getting himself ready for work and the kids ready for school—but I didn't care. My need to be miserable with company was greater than my need to be a good wife and mother. When he answered the phone, I couldn't even say hello.

"Babe," he said, "I'm going to call you back the second I get in the car, okay?"

I nodded my head, as if he could see me, then hung up. I kept on crying until he called me back a half hour later and then reined it in once he put the kids on the phone, then continued crying after they said good-bye. I must have had a shower, although I don't know who helped me with it, and I must have dried my hair and eaten my yogurt and taken my pills, but I don't remember. It was eleven before I finally got dressed. The day was running away from me and I had accomplished exactly nothing except flushing a seemingly inexhaustible pool of tears. And then two familiar voices rang out from behind the curtain.

"Ruth? It's Dr. Zimcik and Dr. Emm. Can we come in?"

I was sitting on my bed, my dopey legs hanging over the side. They felt so heavy they threatened to pull the rest of me down with them. I wanted everyone out of the room so I could continue with my full schedule of crying.

"How are you?" Dr. Zimcik asked.

"Okay."

They both looked at me with doctorly sympathy.

"I'm having a bit of a moment," I admitted.

Dr. Emm took one step closer to my bed. Her job, as far as I could tell, was Chief Tickler. She came to my room every few days with a feather and a safety pin and then alternately poked and tickled me to see how my nerves were progressing. She also performed the toe test. My job was to close my eyes and guess which direction my toes were being pushed or pulled; I got it wrong every time. But Dr. Emm didn't have her tools with her that day, which made me suspicious.

"How is your bladder?" she asked.

I knew what was coming: They wanted me to do my own ICs. They stayed for a minute to explain that the risk of catching a urinary tract infection grew with the frequency of ICs administered by hands other than my own. *Well*, I wanted to say, *the good news is that since I just recently had sex right here in this bed, I already have a bladder infection, so the joke's on you!* Instead, I pretended not to hear them. They continued to talk to me about bowels and bladders and voiding. I focused on Dr. Zimcik's clothes. I loved how she dressed. Rarely a stitch of makeup but always the cutest tops that showed off her delicate collarbone, necklaces that hit just the right spot on her chest, belts that cinched without strangling, interesting color combinations, and, most inspiring of all, flat shoes that made me mourn a little less the fact that I would never be able to wear high heels again. There was lots of encouraging talk about how, once I was able to perform my own ICs, I could be cleared for a day pass home, but what they didn't know was that I would never cart that IC paraphernalia home with me because I had no intention of working toward such a ridiculously puny goal.

Every few days, Dr. Zimcik was required to ask me what my goals were. Each time, I would roll my eyes.

"I'm supposed to ask you and then write it down," she would say.

"Well, it's stupid."

"I know, I know."

But I played the game because I loved Dr. Zimcik and I wanted her to love me back.

I always gave the same obvious answers: to walk and to get my bodily functions back. I was convinced that once I was able to pee on my own, the rest of my recovery would fall into place. So, no—I would *not* be putting my efforts into learning how to do my own ICs. My efforts would go toward peeing in the toilet, thank you very much.

After they left, I resumed crying, then took a break to go to the gym. On my way there, I saw Derek, a patient from my unit. I turned left to avoid him. He was always trying to catch my eye, engage me in conversation. Once, in a weak moment—both on his part and on mine—he told me that his surgery had been botched. He pounded his thigh with his fist.

"Look at that—dead. My legs are dead! I'd like to kick the shit out of my surgeon."

Tears of frustration sprang to his eyes and then to mine, but I couldn't cope with anyone else's problems. I put my hand on his knee—a knee he couldn't feel—said something consoling, and then rolled quickly back to my room and shut the door.

Once I was sure Derek hadn't seen me, I made my way to the gym and found a staff member to crank me up in the standing frame, and then I just stood there, fixed in place like a bug squished between two panes of glass. I laid out the meager contents of my bag on the black tray attached to the frame. I wasn't actually able to concentrate on anything other than standing without my knees collapsing, but the act of placing my notebook and pen on the tray made me feel productive. I put on my sunglasses, not wanting to bear responsibility for setting off a rehab-wide crying jag, and then I stood for as long as I could before the clamminess and nausea set in.

The first time I had been cranked into a standing position inside the frame, Rich and PT Amanda were with me. The act of being upright after so many weeks of only sitting or lying down left me sweaty and faint. They were watching me so expectantly I didn't want to disappoint them, but I knew that if one of them didn't crank me back down immediately, I would pass out.

I had lasted less than five minutes that first time. So my goal was simply to last longer than five minutes the next time. That constituted my entire work out: wheeling myself to the gym, getting cranked into a standing position—and standing. I rang the bell on the machine to alert someone that I was done. It was the same bell you see on the reception desk in a hotel or in someone's house as an ironic joke. Morgan, the pretty girl who owned several different colored skinny jeans and matching Converse running shoes, cranked me down. I transferred into my wheelchair and rolled as quickly as I could back to my room, where I cried and cried and called Rich again and cried and cried.

"I'm going to come have lunch with you, okay?"

My response: I cried and cried. Then I wheeled myself outside to wait at the picnic table until Rich came to save me. For six years, we lived around the corner from a shop with a sign that read, THE BREAD AND BUTTER: *THE BEST SCHNITZEL IN TORONTO!* We'd never gotten around to testing the claim. Rich placed a brown paper bag on the table and then unwrapped *THE BEST SCHNITZEL IN TORONTO!*

And it was. While I ate it, I thought about my pre-surgery relationship to bread. I had given it up, along with dessert and wine (although the wine part only lasted one day) while on a quest to get skinny. But since being at Lyndhurst, my recipe for survival included *all* bread, *all* dessert, and—in place of wine—copious amounts of Metamucil.

When I finished eating every last crumb, I folded the wrapper and then resumed crying. I missed Rich so much. I missed waking up to him and I missed our Sunday morning walks. I missed the simple joy of wanting something and then standing up and walking across the room or the mall or the field to get it. I even missed schlepping the laundry basket up from the basement. I missed using my body to be cute, missed standing in front of a mirror and posing in a new pair of shoes. I missed dancing with Henry in the living room, missed standing back to back with Joey to gauge how much he had grown. I missed sleeping on my stomach. I wondered if Rich would grow resentful of having to take care of me. And could he possibly still be attracted to me? Maybe attraction is layered. What if the attraction he felt for me was finite, a layer sloughed off with each sad stage of my rehabilitation to which he'd borne witness? Maybe all that remained was one thin, quivering husk ready to fall off at the slightest disturbance.

Eventually, I let Rich go back to work to earn our real bread and butter. I pushed back to my room, exhausted from all the crying, rolled myself onto my bed in the middle of the day, and went to sleep. Almost two hours later, I woke up in a panic and in pain. I hadn't taken any oxycodone since first thing that morning. I was surprised that no nurse had ensured that I got my dose until I remembered that it wasn't their job to chase me down and remind me I was in pain. My physio was set for three fifteen with a new therapist standing in that day for Amanda. I moved as quickly as I could to get ready, which is to say that I moved very slowly. My back felt as if it had been pummeled with oranges. Hot sparks and static lit up my body. I didn't see the point in going to physio—I was useless without my painkillers—but not showing up was not an option.

The PT room was almost empty. Most appointments took place in the morning, and it was almost three thirty, close to quittin' time. The substitute PT, Grace, was sitting on the blue plinth, her knees spread wide with her hands resting on her thighs.

"It's nice to meet you," she said.

"I'm having a very shitty day."

Grace said nothing. Had she heard me? The look on her face was inscrutable. I thought: *If she tries to hug me, I will punch her.*

"Do you want to walk?"

"I don't know how."

She kept her eyes on me as if I might take off but called over her shoulder, "Sarah! Come spot for me!"

I didn't bother looking up again to see who Sarah was, missing the only opportunity I would have to meet her face to face.

"Let's go, Ruth."

I was hauled up out of my wheelchair and pulled somewhat upright. With very little time to process what was happening, I was on my feet, which felt as if they were skimming the surface of water—not quite standing, not quite floating. I never wore shoes in the PT room. Amanda always began our sessions by giving me a quick foot massage, pulling on each of my toes and rubbing my arches to "turn them on." But Grace didn't bother with any of that. Once my shoes were off, I was up. I could feel a presence behind me, a pressure. This was the unseen Sarah. I couldn't tell where her hands were or what they were doing, although I had a very clear image of me as a marionette with Sarah as the master pulling the strings. In front, Grace was half crouched and holding tight to my thighs. I gripped her shoulders for support. Whatever pain I had been experiencing when I arrived had either disappeared or gone into hiding when faced with these two tiny Amazons.

"Left knee, left bum! Right knee, right bum!" Grace barked.

"Do I look like a joke?" I yelled. I felt as if I were battling forces so fierce, the only way to get through it was to be very loud. "I don't want to look like a joke!"

"You look good. Now stop thinking and *walk*!"

"Am I hurting you?" I asked Grace, who, I learned, was five months pregnant.

"No," she said, even though she was sweating. "Go! Pretend you're keeping up with your kids."

I didn't dare look at my feet. Not since the surgery had I put such blind faith in a stranger. I figured that if I wasn't falling, then I must have been doing something right. I must have been touching the ground, although I couldn't really feel it. I sensed a pressure on my heels but not on my toes. Momentum and determination—Grace's and Sarah's more than mine—propelled me around the room. *All I have to do*, I told myself, *is make it back to my wheelchair*. When I did, I flopped into it, breathing heavily.

"Okay," Grace said, catching her breath, too. "How did that feel?"

I couldn't answer.

"Those better be happy tears," she said.

I nodded my head and then I called Rich.

"I WALKED!" I screamed into the phone.

Within minutes, he had sent out a mass email with the subject line: *She Walked*.

●

"This is a problem," I told Rich the following day when I received multiple texts, emails, and phone calls from people who believed that the struggle was over and I was back to my old walking self again.

"But you *did* walk," Rich said.

"Not on my own, babe. I was basically yanked around the PT room by two surprisingly small women. You can't tell people I'm walking."

"But you walked."

"Not really, Rich."

"I told people you walked because you walked. You did."

"Honey."

"You walked."

"Okay."

My surgeon cousin Joel popped by a couple of days later. He found me in the gym, pinned inside the standing frame. I dinged my call bell and Morgan hauled the lever and lowered me back to the ground. Joel and I went back to my room, where I showed off the homework he had texted me to do: rub my right foot against my left leg from knee to ankle; repeat on opposite side; tap my toes on the floor ten times with each foot.

"See?" I said. "I can do all of it." Granted, it looked loopier on the left side than on the right, my foot waving around drunkenly before touching down. I was so focused on my feet that I didn't notice Joel disappear behind my chair. He shoved his hands underneath my armpits to pull me upright.

"What the hell are you doing?"

"Let's see you walk."

"Are you crazy?! Joel, I'm scared—put me down!"

My feet skittered around the floor, blindly searching for a toehold.

"I won't drop you, I promise. I just want to see where you're at."

"Joel!"

"Just try."

I moved like dead weight. Was this how I walked with Grace and Sarah, I wondered? With them I felt airborne, euphoric, like I could do anything. With Joel I flopped around my room like a ragdoll. I could hear him trying not to grunt. I knew he was testing more than just my strength. He needed to see how successful the surgery was, how well he had taught his friend and fellow, the neurosurgeon Dr. Ginsberg. I could see that he was feeling personally responsible for my progress.

"That's enough, Joel. Put me back in my chair."

He lowered me down and then took a step back. We were both winded.

"So?" I asked.

"Your right leg is strong—it'll be fine. It will probably take your left leg longer to catch up. You might be left with a little shuffle."

He demonstrated with his hand what he saw when my leg was in motion: like cleaning a table with a sponge, a gentle circular movement. Something shifted in my stomach. I had seen people walk like that, with that draggy leg, the very definition of lame.

"Well, that most certainly will not be happening to me," I said, pulling myself up tall.

He shrugged.

"I am not going to shuffle, Joel!" I yelled.

After he left, I allowed myself to feel furious for a while and then I made a decision: It was time to supplement my physio with some outside help. I knew just who to ask.

I had met Sal, a private physiotherapist from outside Lyndhurst, while he was working with The Captain, a patient in the only other private room in our unit. Sightings of The Captain were rare—he complied with the only mandatory patient requirement, which was to show up for physio for one hour a day. Otherwise, he stayed in his room until Sal came knocking. It seemed clear that, given the droves of visitors he had and the catered dinners that arrived daily for him and his family, The Captain knew all the right people. If PT Sal was good enough for The Captain, then he might be good enough for me, too. Without much thought, research, or consultation, I hired him.

We didn't settle into a groove right away, but I had learned that first impressions in this strange new land couldn't always be trusted. Even Dr. Asshole, my nemesis from the hospital, proved to be a more complex character than I had originally thought. Three hours into surgery, it was Dr. Asshole who was the messenger sent to speak to Rich about my progress.

"You mean *that* guy, the toe-tester guy? Was he in my surgery?" I asked Rich.

"I don't know. I didn't ask."

"Was he nice to you?"

"He was okay." It pained him to admit this.

"But we hated that guy!"

"I know."

"I *liked* hating that guy." I sighed. "Now I can't hate that guy."

"Me neither."

Sal had just bought a new house and was looking forward to the arrival of his first baby. His wife was seven months pregnant and he talked a fair bit about how that was affecting both of them. He told me about his furniture shopping trips, proudly name-checking all the brands. I tried to keep up with his banter, but it was hard to concentrate on anything other than where my leg was, which was often hoisted at a ninety-degree angle with my foot resting on a chair, making me look like a drunken heron. Sal's hands were strong and I felt confident he wouldn't let me fall, but it didn't mean I could hold his poses forever. My right leg quivered and swayed, threatening to give out. I wanted to ask him what I should be concentrating on, what I should feel "activating," but Sal had moved from talk of furniture to talk of renovation.

"Okay, I feel more than buzzing now," I cut in. "My leg is stinging." Sal gently lowered my leg to the ground.

"You should know," he said, "your nerves *will* get worse before they get better."

This news flash didn't scare me—in fact, I took it as a good sign, since at that moment my leg had never felt worse. After a few more sessions, Sal encouraged me to get out of the hospital and come to his spinal cord rehab gym. This seemed like a good idea.

On the day I went to Sal's gym, I had already completed a morning PT session with Amanda and I was exhausted. When I was first admitted to Lyndhurst, it struck me as absurd that in a twenty-four-hour day, only one hour was devoted to actual physical therapy. Surely I could handle more than that, I thought. But after each session, it was all I could do to stay awake long enough to wheel myself back to my room.

Sal's gym looked much like Lyndhurst's, but with less activity. I was the sole patient there, which meant Sal could fill the space with more talk of all the things he and his wife were planning in their rush to get ready for the baby. He was moved by the way his wife's body was changing and this made me feel a surge of warmth toward him. He laughed a little recalling the long skirt his wife had been favoring and which she wore with her Birkenstocks. As her belly pushed all her other clothes out of rotation, this particular outfit was proving to be the go-to.

"I told her she looked like a Jew." Sal laughed. He was pulling on my clueless toes, trying to activate them.

"Like a what?" I asked.

"Like a Jew."

I didn't tell him I was Jewish. I'm sure he would have apologized, but I was so tired, so done for the day, I couldn't summon the strength to get into it. I concentrated as hard as I could on his instructions, which meant that I became very quiet, but because I had already established myself as the chatty sort, my quietness proved to be unsettling. I could sense Sal trying to figure out how things had gone off the rails. I felt bad for him and also mad at myself for disrupting the tone of our appointment.

"I think you're ready to try stairs," Sal said, switching gears. We made our way to the nearest staircase. He was beside me, encouraging me, trying to get things back on track. I locked my chair into place and then tried to stand on my own. I gripped the banister while Sal used his hands to manipulate my legs into a walking motion, but I couldn't get my foot to move in concert with my knee and my thigh and my glutes. Frustration burned through my body. Sal's words swirled. I stopped listening and started thinking about how distressing the ride over had been, how my cabdriver had hopped out to help me, how he had leaned into my chair to push it up the ramp in the back of the specially outfitted taxi. He anchored my chair to the floor and pulled a seatbelt tight around both the chair and me so that I was fixed in place. My purse sat primly on my lap, my hands folded over it. When he was finished fussing, he took the driver's seat and told me how he was a hand healer back in his country, and that he felt strongly that the key to my recovery was swimming. Given the healing properties I experienced daily in the shower, I wanted to pursue this conversation, but I had been far too preoccupied with getting to Sal's gym in one piece. And now I was tired, mad at myself for being so naïve as to think I could do two rounds of physio in one day, and dreading the drive back.

As the hour wound down, I saw my taxi driver backing his car up to the end of the wheelchair ramp. I thanked Sal, who had also run out of steam. I sat as straight as I could while the driver bolted and belted me into place. I was tight-lipped for the entire ride back, unable to eke out even the most benign mm-hmms to the story he was telling me. When we got back to Lyndhurst, the security guard at reception saluted me and I saluted him, but I didn't stop for our usual chat. I went straight to my room, transferred to my bed, lay on my side facing the window, and cried until it was dark. It wasn't Sal that upset me. I knew he was a decent guy preoccupied with the wonderful changes about to happen to his family. I was upset because I could remember with greater clarity how it felt to be pregnant than how it felt to walk.

9

Step 4—Be the Mom

"Do your drugs make you high?" my girlfriend Joanie asked me in a whisper one afternoon.

It was a perfectly reasonable question that I met with a frat-house response: "I wish."

Prior to the surgery, narcotics played a very minor role in my life. I only took Ativan to fly, and on those rare occasions when my stress level manifested in a thumping heart that became too percussive to ignore. Post-surgery, however, I was amazed at the ease with which I cycled through my drugs: morphine, Percocet, oxycodone. Though frightening and evocative, they were necessary. The pain in my back was so thick, so seemingly impenetrable, the drugs barely took the edge off, let alone made me feel good. For this, I was profoundly grateful. I never requested more than my prescribed amount, not because I'm a martyr but because I'm a chicken. The constipation that followed was simply not worth the extra measure of pain relief. I started cutting down on my dosage in the hopes that I would be rewarded with a more smoothly running digestive system, but was furious when my body refused to cooperate. I noticed, however, that the decrease in my oxycodone didn't really cause an increase in pain. Very quickly, I weaned my-self down to just one dose a day—before I went to sleep. I called my cousin Joel to brag.

"Taking just one a day is useless," he said. "Stop taking them, period."

So I did what he said, and it was like falling off a cliff.

I was up the entire night. I lay there, counting backward from a hundred, trying to ignore the riot that had broken out in every single part of my body, until it occurred to me that I didn't *have* to just lie there—maybe it was time to start reading again. I found a book on my Kindle, bought it, became engrossed in it, and read right up to the part where the mother thinks she is pregnant again only to learn that her pregnancy is actually ovarian cancer. She dies a few pages later.

I was ten days late for my period. I had told one of my nurses and she joked that maybe I was pregnant. I laughed off the absurdity—I was forty-seven and Rich had had a vasectomy years ago. Still, I added up the symptoms: nausea, no period, bloating, headaches. I went to the Internet and cross-referenced my symptoms with those of ovarian cancer. By the time Dr. Zimcik came to see me the following day, my nerves were rattled beyond anything gabapentin could con-trol. I barely had time to register her pink pants and black-and-white polka-dot shirt before I cried out, "I think I have ovarian cancer!"

"Okay," she said, cocking her head to the side. "I'm not going to tell you you're crazy because what you already have is exceed-ingly rare, but I will tell you this: I am more likely to win the lot-tery tonight than you are to have ovarian cancer."

She stood up, looking for something. "Where are the gloves in here?"

"In the bathroom."

She disappeared and came back in seconds. She moved quickly and brightly, like a polka-dot firefly.

"Would it make you feel better if I did a pelvic exam right now?"

"Yes."

"Okay. Just lay back."

She felt my cervix, my uterus, my ovaries, but her probing fingers barely registered.

"It all seems really good, Ruth."

Why is it so hard not to cry when a doctor says your name? I wanted to hug her, but I knew how pathetic that would look.

"You've been through a lot," she said, standing up to go. "You can tell me anything and I'll listen."

"I think you're wonderful!"

There. Not nearly as pathetic as a hug.

•

October crept in, tiptoeing around me. I called Joey.

"Hey, honey—just need to confirm something. Is the date I'm seeing on the calendar really real?"

He sighed heavily through the phone.

It was my own fault for trying to be cute when there was nothing cute about my absence. This little joke probably wouldn't have worked even if I had delivered it while standing in our kitchen making dinner, but at least I would have been standing and at least I would have been making dinner. Some of my best and most heartfelt exchanges with Joey were by text, but on the phone it was a different story, and in person, even worse. He could barely look at me when he came to visit. His grades had slipped. Rich and Joey were arguing a lot. It was a perfect storm of absent mother, overwhelmed father, and teenage angst.

Texting was also the perfect way for me to be a busybody. From my bed, I tried to control the kids' after-school schedules even though Rich sorted everything out each morning. Invariably, this caused confusion. It also made Rich crazy.

"But I want to help," I explained to him.

"I know you want to help, but that's not your job right now. Your job is to get better. *I've got this.*"

In other words, my family was getting on fine without me. I'd already noted how some of Rich's pronouns had changed (he talked about Henry coming into *his* bed to sleep with him), and how other pronouns had been excised altogether (*my* car had become *the* car). I was at the mercy of my drunken feet. Until I could get them under control, I would not get the keys to my car or my household back.

"How is my Henry doing?" I asked Rich one day.

"He's okay."

"Does he miss me?"

"Of course he does. We all do."

"Has he asked you any questions about me?"

"He came to my bedroom door the other night and asked when you were coming home."

"Oh no."

"Then he had a little cry."

Henry and I are both Geminis, which is the only sign about which I have even a passing knowledge. We are apparently a *joy* to those around us. We are also loyal friends, and have emotions that can turn on a dime. I would hate to live with me, but I hated living without Henry. I had been worried about the effect of my surgery on him, but when he came for visits, he seemed excited. He would sit on my lap while Rich pushed us around outside, or he would hang out at the back of my wheelchair with his arms wrapped around my neck, or coax me out of my chair so he could it use it to do wheelies.

Early on in my stay, he said to me: "You have to admit, Mom. This *is* kind of fun." But the novelty of my being away had finally worn off. With my recovery on an uptick and the limits of my freedom slowly expanding, it felt like the right time to set up a new after-school schedule—one that could be accomplished without stepping on anyone's toes.

I called them my one-on-ones, and my first was with Joey. I suggested that I wheel down and meet him at Starbucks, just a few blocks away from Lyndhurst. I had forged a pretty decent relationship with my chair, one I couldn't have foreseen even two weeks earlier when I sob-yelled to Dr. Zimcik that I was *not leaving this hospital in a wheelchair!* She had fixed me with one of her enigmatic close-mouthed smiles.

"Ruth," she said, waiting until I looked at her before continuing. "Do you see anyone here teaching you wheelchair skills?"

"I'm just telling you right now. I am not leaving here in a goddamn wheelchair!"

"Of *course* you're not."

I had to look away. She had the power to distract me with her amazing accessories, and I didn't want to be distracted. It was probably the worst-kept secret in my unit that Dr. Zimcik was my girl-crush. I didn't need to be in therapy to know I was experiencing transference. Rumy was an angel, but with Dr. Zimcik, I felt an instant kinship. She swore like a teenage boy. She was honest but also sensitive. She lived in the same area I lived when my kids were the same ages as her little kids. Day after day, she was able to talk me down from whatever tree I had managed to get myself stuck in. She didn't reciprocate my feelings; she just accepted them.

"And anyway," said Dr. Zimcik, trying to ease me back to a calmer state, "you need your chair to get your apples from Neville."

"Good point."

Meeting with Joey meant leaving Lyndhurst unaccompanied for the first time. Getting to the gates just beyond the hospital's circular drive was a breeze. Henry's words had had an effect on me: It *was* fun, especially when the road sloped down and I could coast as if I were on my bike.

I got as far as the first stop sign before deciding the more prudent thing to do was to get off the road. I used extra arm strength to get myself over the lip of a driveway to ensure I made it up onto the sidewalk without rolling backward, but I pushed with too much gusto and narrowly avoided a face plant with a curbside sapling. Rolling on the sidewalk proved more treacherous than the road. There were obstacles everywhere: poorly placed garbage cans, break-your-mama's-back cracks that made me veer off course, piles of leaves. Cars blew past me and I ducked. The joy of heading out on my own had been swallowed up by the wind that was now shaking my chair, trying to dislodge me. Joey called me on my cell. I could hear him but he couldn't hear me.

"Where are you?" he was asking.

"I'm right here!" I yelled. "In the wind!"

"Mom? Mom? Are you there?"

I sent a frantic "Help me!" text and then saw him running toward me with his red knapsack slapping his back.

We made it to Starbucks safely, where we sat and talked like old pals. He didn't look at his phone and he didn't roll his eyes at me once. I bought him a Frappuccino and a lemon poppy seed loaf, feeling like a divorced parent who buys her children whatever they want out of guilt.

"What's the most difficult part of high school so far?" I asked him.

He shrugged. "Nothing, I guess."

I wanted to ask him if the most difficult part was me not being around.

"Is it hard?"

"Is what hard?"

"Science."

He shrugged.

"Math?"

"Eh."

"English?"

"Really, Mom?"

"You do have impeccable grammar."

"Of course I do. I wrote a new joke."

"Tell me!"

"It's a medical one."

"Go on."

"Why did the guy get rid of his tapeworm?"

"Why?"

"It was getting under his skin."

"Ha! Nice one, Joe!"

I picked at the crumbs of his lemon poppy seed loaf. "Are you sleeping okay?"

"That's a weird question, Mom."

At three thirty in the morning, my worst fears came out to play in a field of crashed cars and bloodied swimming pools, broken locks and mangled bikes—all worst-case events I couldn't control. But it was daytime now, the weather was fine, my son was okay.

"That *was* a totally weird question. Honey, I have to get back for my next round of pharmaceuticals. Care to push me?"

Not being particularly mindful of my fragility—or maybe he was just having fun—Joey decided to gun it. I forgot about this one curb, the one that everyone got hung up on when they wheeled me to Starbucks. It was more step than bump. A good mountain bike could have taken it easily, but not a wheelchair. Joey ran straight at it. The wheels slammed into the curb. I clutched the arms of my chair but still flung forward. Pine needles from passing trees grazed my forehead before I flopped back down into my seat.

"Whoa!"

"Are you all right?" asked a guy walking past.

"I'm good I'm good," I puffed.

"Sorry! Sorry, Mom!"

"Actually, would you mind helping us out?"

The stranger gently tilted me backward and got me up and over the curb. I felt like a nineteenth-century lady who needed a man's arm to step over horse dung.

"Thank you so much!" Joey said, white-faced with relief.

"That's his good deed for the day. Now, don't *ever* fly me over a curb again!"

Two days later, the boys' nanny, Ellen, drove over with Henry for his one-on-one. It was my first time meeting her, although I spoke to her on the phone practically every day.

"The boys really like you," I told her.

"Thank you. I really like them. They're good boys."

"You're doing a great job. I don't know what we'd do without you." I wanted to say more but I couldn't. Ellen put down her newspaper and bag of chips to come over and hug me. "You're going to make me cry," she whispered.

"Don't do that because then I'll start crying and I have a date with my son."

"You ready, Mom?" Henry asked.

"Ready!"

Instead of Starbucks, we wheeled over to Tim Hortons at the Holland Bloorview Kids Rehabilitation Hospital next door. The going was much smoother—no bumps, no cracks, no cars. I could have wheeled myself, but Henry insisted on pushing me. He whispered in my ear: "There's a new song on the radio that I really like. Can I sing it to you while I push?"

"Of course!"

"I may not get all the words right."

He sang quietly and I tipped my head back to hear—a new song by Adam Levine.

We got to Tim Hortons and parked at a table near the window. The foyer was flooded with sunlight and children. The kids, both able and disabled, didn't look twice at me; they were used to people in wheelchairs. As with Joey, I let Henry have whatever he wanted.

"Did you want something, too, Mom?"

"I'd love a cup of tea but you'll have to carry it, okay?"

"Sure."

I watched him as he walked slowly with our snacks and drinks, his eyes never leaving the cup of hot tea. He didn't have to glance down at his feet to see where they were. It was hard to imagine ever having that ease with my body again, but I *did* imagine it. In the absence of normal feeling in my entire bottom half, I made it my job to imagine what my life was going to look like when I finally left rehab; how I would cope with everything from lifting a hot pot off the stove to putting my pants on.

Henry sat down and I asked a lot of questions. I had nowhere else to be; it was just me and my boy.

He might have grown used to seeing adults in wheelchairs, adjusting the parameters of his comfort zone to accommodate them, but children in wheelchairs were a different story for both of us. We were conscious of keeping our eyelines tight to each other. We finished our snacks and wheeled back to Lyndhurst, the cold pushing us faster than I wanted to go.

"We'll do this every week until I come home, okay, Hank?"

He nodded.

"Every Tuesday and Thursday. You and Joey can pick whichever day you want, plus our dinners and our weekends, of course."

I was rushing, as if Henry was already on the train and the train was chugging out of the station.

Back in my room, I looked at myself in the mirror. My heart began a slow thud. I had a question and I needed to ask it out loud, the one question that no one dared ask me, the one question I was afraid to ask myself:

What if I really never walk again?

I waited for the answer while looking into my own unblinking eyes. I felt restless. My mind paced where my legs couldn't. It bothered me that I didn't know the song Henry had sung to me—I was used to being up to date with all the new songs on the radio. The chorus rang in my ears. If I had been home at that time of day, the music would have been cranked up while I made dinner: Jack Johnson, Joss Stone, Nikka Costa.

I opened the top drawer of my dresser and took my computer out of its black sleeve. I scrolled to my unused iTunes page looking for the song Henry had sung, pressing some buttons without much result. I was done with the sounds of the hospital acting as the soundtrack to my life; I called Joey.

"You need to teach me how to steal songs from YouTube."

I downloaded every single song I could think of that my feet could reasonably keep time to. Then I blasted Michael Jackson out of my computer. All the old stuff: "ABC," "I Want You Back," "Shake Your Body (Down to the Ground)," "Rock with You." My feet were keeping the beat and my hands were up in the air. I was amazed at how coordinated I was—even my left foot didn't lose time. Joy zapped through my body, forging new neuropathic highways. For entire songs I was able to ignore the strangled sensation behind my knees, the sandbag heaviness of my calves, the pebbly feeling in the soles of my feet, the burning sensation in my bum, the zizzy feeling in my thighs. For a while I forgot how frustrated I was. I didn't close my curtains. I turned up the volume. In no time at all, a male figure appeared at my door. Even in profile, I knew who it was: Derek.

"Hey!" I called out to his reflection. He jerked his head up in surprise and then boldly looked inside my room.

"Is the music too loud?"

"Oh, no, no. Not at all. I like it."

"I like it, too. This place needs a little funky-funk, don't you think?"

"Oh, sure, sure."

By purposely keeping my door open and playing music loud enough for the whole unit to hear, it looked as if I were sending an invitation when really, I just wanted to block out the other sounds of rehab. But he was still a dude and I was still a married woman and I wasn't about to invite him in for a handful of jujubes and a nightcap of Metamucil.

"Anyhow, Derek, I'm kind of winding down now. I'll see you tomorrow, I guess."

"Oh, right, right."

Like always, he took his cue quickly and wheeled away.

Later that night, Rumy came to my room, her face filled with mischief. She sang, "Guess who has a crush on you?"

"Derek," I said.

She was disappointed—I had stolen her news. "How did you know?"

I lifted one shoulder. "He follows me around a little."

"He said to me: *Oh that Ruth, she's so pretty.*"

I had never looked worse in my life. I felt so beaten down and desexualized by the whole hospital experience, it was a wonder that anyone—my husband included, my husband *especially*— could look at me with anything like desire. The last thing I wanted Rumy to know was that this shaggy-haired hippie with the gray goatee and the biker vibe had single-handedly made me feel like the hottest girl in school.

10

Progress, Practice Makes Perfect

There were only two floors at Lyndhurst but I always pressed the wrong elevator button. My room was on the second floor—I thought it was the first. Physio was on the first floor—I thought it was the second. Like my toe test, I got it wrong every time. I could tell that my mother, a self-diagnosed "number dyslexic," got a neat kick out of my up/down confusion. This should have been the perfect opportunity for her to get back at me for all the times I pointed out her lapses in memory, her screwups of times and dates, even her repetition of stories, but she never did. She was the first person to text me most days, often before six A.M. Little messages: *Are you awake, darling? How are you?* She knew how difficult mornings were for me. But I never answered her texts right away. I didn't want her to know that I *was* awake, that I *did* need contact, that I felt horribly, inconsolably alone.

In the struggle to work out the ratio of who to dump more of my sadness onto, my mom or my husband, I had to ask myself, Who could handle it more? It was no contest. I offloaded my angst onto my mother every chance I got.

"Maybe we should come up with a schedule to come visit you?" my mom suggested.

"No."

"I think your father and I should come every other day."

"No! That's ridiculous. I'm not making a schedule. I *have* a schedule. I don't *need* another schedule."

"Some of our friends would like to call you."

"No!"

"But they're worried about you."

"That's very nice, but no, they can't call."

My mother became very quiet.

"They can text if they want."

"Larry!" My mom yelled to my father, who must have been in the next room. "Ruthie says our friends can text her!"

"Tell her that's a good idea!" I heard my father yell back.

"Oh, thank you, Ruthie!" my mom said. "That's an excellent idea!"

I cringed at how little it took to make her and my father happy; and also how little it took to upend their day. I might have been quick to snap but I was slow to reveal true neediness. When I was feeling particularly awful, I wouldn't answer my phone, not trusting myself not to break into tears when I heard their voices. Instead, I would send out a text: *Feeling a little low today. Will call tomorrow.*

In front of the elevators in my unit one day, trying to figure out whether I had to go up or down to get to the lobby, I decided to never again rib my mother over not getting the dates or times or years of things right. I would have happily traded my body confusion for her number confusion any day. I was just about to text her something funny when I came wheel to wheel with Kellan, the hospital spokesman for the Canadian Paraplegic Association. I had barely seen him since he had burst into my room several weeks earlier, CPA folder on his lap. I had calmed down considerably since that day. To show him there were no hard feelings, I said hello first. He nodded and then paid a lot of attention to the closed elevator doors. Once inside, he pressed "down."

"Could you press two, please?" I asked.

"We're on two," he said.

"God, I'm dumb. I meant down, which you did. You pressed down. Thanks."

The elevator doors opened, and Kellan rolled away. But as I met my friends Jeff and Kathy in the lobby, Kellan stayed on my mind, so much so that I was still thinking about him when the three of us went back to my room. I told my friends the story of Kellan and our fraught conversation from weeks earlier. And then I remembered what a show I had made of moving my legs around when he came to my room to "recruit" me to his association; how I had gathered my knees to me, wiggled my toes, crossed my feet back and forth without caring if they got tangled up in each other—which they did; how I had waved my knees, then clacked them together even though it hurt a little and I didn't mean for them to actually touch. My thinking was that if Kellan could see how clearly *un*-paralyzed I was, then he would take his little Association bible with its forecasts of all the joys I could still count as a newly-minted wheelie and stick it someplace highly unpleasant.

I finished my story and felt instantly awful; I couldn't even look at my friends. Kellan came to see me that day because that was his *job*: to offer support to new patients and open their eyes to an alternative life. He had done the right thing, it just wasn't the right thing for me.

Jeff stood up and was scanning my room.

"Where is it?" he asked.

"Where is what?"

"The folder that guy gave you."

I pointed to the windowsill where I had tossed it. Jeff strode over and grabbed the folder. He tried to rip it in half, but the laminate cover slipped in his hands. He strode back across the room and jammed it into the garbage can by my bed. Then, even though his foot barely fit inside the shallow can, he stomped on it.

"Done," he said. "Want me to get rid of those dead flowers, too?"

•

I loved having visitors—it was my favorite part of every day. In my real life I was quite social, but I also guarded my own company carefully. I enjoyed the solitary routines of my day. I was good at making busywork when work wasn't busy enough. I enjoyed running errands and ticking things off my list and sneaking to the mall on my own to buy things I knew I would probably return the next day, ensuring that the cycle of make-busywork continued. But inevitably, after a few days of this, I would start to feel strange, the symptoms piling up until the diagnosis was clear: loneliness. And then I'd start making calls: request for company, please.

But at Lyndhurst, I needed something social to look forward to every day. Lunchtime was my happy hour, when guests would most often visit. I had only one strict proviso: If you come for lunch, you bring the lunch. I wasn't fussy about what we ate. In fact, I looked forward to the big reveal. Lunch, something I used to eat from a container while standing in my kitchen doing the crossword, was now an event worth dressing up *and* sitting down for. I would wait with anticipation, my all-purpose table lowered to lunch position. My guest and I would sit across from each other with our feast (sushi, Tim Hortons sandwiches, Thai food, homemade sandwiches, fresh salads) spread out over every cramped inch of my tray table and for that hour, in the eyes of those I loved, my old life was reflected back to me with a glimpse of my future self layered underneath. No one asked the unanswerable questions: How long would I be in rehab? Would I ever work again? Would I ever walk again? And no one, or almost no one, cried.

My friend Laura came for a visit one afternoon. Her smile was wobbly and tentative from the start. I had been at Lyndhurst for some time already, so I had forgotten how jarring it was for friends seeing me for the first time. Not long after she arrived, my body started to rebel. My bum was thick with pins and needles. I needed to lie on my right side to find some relief. Laura watched while I gracelessly transferred out of my chair and onto my bed. Once there, I had to face away from her to relieve the growing buildup of static in my left thigh.

"How about you move your chair over here so I can see you," I said.

But Laura wanted to sit on the bed with me. I picked up my legs and carefully moved them to make room for her.

"Would you like me to rub your feet?" she asked, shyly.

"Sure!"

My enthusiasm was a lie. I hated having my feet touched. Each morning, before my physio session, Amanda would massage my feet and yank on my toes to activate them. I was able to handle this with the help of deep breathing and the knowledge that it was for my own good, but to anyone else, my feet were off limits. My feet even hated it when *I* touched them. And then there were the blasted visits from Dr. Emm, the physiatrist, who randomly popped by with her safety pins and feathers. Rich's business partner, wanting to do something nice for me, asked if she could dispatch someone to Lyndhurst to give me a foot massage and a pedicure.

"No!" I screamed into the phone, as if the pedicurist/sadist were right outside my door packing hot stones and cuticle pushers.

I looked at Laura as she dug her thumbs into my arches. She was crying.

"Oh, honey," I said. "Laura—it's okay. I'm going to be okay, really. Just keep rubbing my feet."

I empathized with her helplessness, but I did so from a removed place. I was not sad for myself. I felt like a Jenga puzzle—so many pieces of my previous self had been removed, and yet I hadn't toppled.

And that's when I found the answer to the question, *What if I never walk again?* I would be okay. Even if it remained unclear what form "okay" would take, I would be okay.

The days were getting shorter, crisper. I didn't want to still be at Lyndhurst when it was too cold to sit outside at the picnic table. I couldn't bear the thought of being trapped inside, wearing heavier sweaters and slippers. It was time for me to make peace with socks. It was time to get out of my chair.

•

Six months earlier, during my Jewish choir practice, my fellow soprano had suggested I call her magical chiropractor when I complained about my tingling feet. I ended up seeing him several times. Dr. Magic, while unable to pinpoint exactly what my problem was, presciently recognized that the bottom half of my body wasn't listening to the top half. He encouraged me to walk on grass in my bare feet as often as possible. He seemed to intuit that my body needed grounding.

"Stand close to a tree," he said.

"Are you suggesting that I *hug* a tree, Dr. Magic?"

He shrugged as if to say: *can't hurt.*

The standing frame inside the gym had helped me get over the first hurdle—standing up without throwing up. The next hurdle was to figure out how to stand in a relaxed position outside the safety of the standing frame, on the grass, by my picnic table. Too often, I overcompensated for the muddled sensation behind my legs by overextending my knees. I had assumed that the moment I felt the stretch behind my legs it meant I had comfortably risen to my full height. One look in the mirror would have told a different story: I looked like a demented soldier.

"Soften your knees," Amanda instructed over and over with a light tap to the back of my legs.

The tap was unspeakably irritating. Adding to my frustration was the fact that I couldn't figure out where the tap was happening. A scratch on the top of my foot might register on my heel, while stubbing my big toe made my baby toe curl in pain. But I took my lessons with Amanda seriously and tried to apply them to real life, which meant spending hours outside standing up, then sitting down. It was like being in synagogue.

"Rei!" I yelled to my fellow patient as he walked my way. "Check me out!"

He was the only patient who refused to buy into my no-eye-contact shtick. He was always smiling and always moving and always alone. He wore his hair in a Dorothy Hamill bowl cut, which I was certain owed more to the lack of salon services at Lyndhurst than to a secret love of the 1970s.

He limped over with his cane, dragging his right foot.

I stood there, meaningfully, before plopping back into my seat. "I did it! Ten seconds standing up! Whooo!"

He smiled. "That's how I started, too." He spoke slowly, like a sensei.

"I was told not to try any of this stuff outside on my own."

"Uh-huh," he said. "Me, too."

"I guess they're afraid we'll topple over and then sue their asses," I said.

He laughed. "Oh well. You have to try, right?"

"It seems to me the worst thing has happened already, anyway."

Rei didn't say anything. I knew some of his story, although I couldn't remember how I knew—a car crash, a foreign country, friends, some of them dead—but we didn't talk about it. I don't think he knew anything about me, but I couldn't be sure. Fragments of patients' stories were scattered throughout Lyndhurst. We only had to look beyond the tracks of our own wheelchairs to find them.

"I can't believe how well *you're* walking," I said.

Rei picked up his pant leg with his good hand and showed me the band he wore over his calf and under his foot. "I do what I can. I watch you out here. You work so hard."

"We all do."

Most patients' stories happened under such ordinary circumstances, they made the end result that much more devastating: a slip in the kitchen while making dinner; a too-fast ATV ride in the country; tumbling off the gutter on a gorgeous fall day; blacking out in the bathroom; so many motorcycle accidents. They were all perfect candidates for magical thinking: *If I hadn't done* this, *if only I'd done* that. My injury didn't qualify for magical thinking—I didn't go looking for trouble. Trouble found me. It also found Arpita.

I met her in the gym, pulled upright in the standing frame next to mine. Out of the corner of my eye, I saw her looking at me, but I refused to look back. She asked me a couple of questions and I gave her short answers before returning to what I was doing, which was the exact same thing she was doing: standing there, locked into position, looking out over the gym, trying to figure out where in space her body was.

Arpita had a nice face and huge brown eyes behind her oversized glasses. I decided to make an exception to my no-engagement rule.

"I was driving home from work one day," she told me, even though I hadn't asked her a question. "My legs started to feel tingly, then numb, then nothing at all in such a short span of time that I had to pull over and call my husband to come and get me. I couldn't drive. I couldn't feel the pedals. It's been months now and I still have no feeling in my legs."

"I'm so sorry," I said.

"Yes. Every day, my husband drives here from Mississauga to give me an hour-and-a-half body massage."

"Every day, really?" I asked.

"Every single day, yes."

She was wearing sweatpants, like everyone else at Lyndhurst. I could see that her bottom was quite puffy. I knew what that meant. I stared straight ahead, concentrating hard, as if I were driving in a blizzard.

"What happened to you?" she asked.

"Tumor."

"Can you feel anything now?"

I didn't want to upset her by admitting that I did have some feeling—however foreign that feeling was—but I also didn't want to lie. I felt I owed my body respect for the work it had been doing.

"A little bit," I said.

"Can you pee?"

"Sometimes."

"I can't." She paused. "I can't do . . . either." She looked behind her at her puffy bum. "I have to wear a di-a-per." She pronounced the word in three distinct syllables.

"That must be really hard," I said.

"So hard," she said, and looked down. "So hard."

She also had two boys, the same ages as Joey and Henry. Even with the teenage angst starting to kick up a storm in our house before the surgery, Rich and I were in the golden age of parenting—a time when we could decide at the last second that we wanted to go out for dinner without having to scramble for a babysitter, when we could let our kids hop on their bikes and go for a ride without standing in the driveway, arms crossed over our chests, making sure they looked both ways before crossing the street. While their moods were unpredictable, their love for us wasn't. The hugs still came even when they thought they didn't need them, and sometimes, when they came down to breakfast in the morning, their feet looked measurably bigger. I looked at Arpita and she looked at me. We were united in missing all that; we didn't need to say it.

Once I'd broken the ice with Arpita, I realized there was one other patient I was hoping to meet. I had been surreptitiously tracking Carmen, whose progress appeared to be running along similar lines to mine. She looked about my age, maybe a little younger. I first noticed her in her wheelchair. Sometimes we were in the PT room at the same time, sometimes in the gym at the same time. She was always—quite literally—just a few steps ahead of me. I noticed her on the treadmill, when she advanced to two sticks, and when she took slow walks around the back of the facility where I sat at my picnic table. I would eat my apple and watch her. Sometimes we caught each other's eye, then smiled shyly like one of us might ask the other one out. I liked her, even without a word shared between us. I felt invested in her progress, and oddly, I trusted her. So one day, after I had scored a seat at the tiny biped cafeteria outside the in-patient dining hall, I asked if she wanted to join me in eating a bag of chips. She did, which was when I learned that our beginnings were remarkably similar—tingly feet, persistent numbness, multiple visits with doctors, MRIs, months of anxiety, and then a spinal meningioma diagnosis.

"I can't believe it," I said. "It's like meeting my twin. The odds of having what we had are literally one in a million, and here we are, the two of us, sitting at the same table."

"Did you have a laminectomy?" she asked.

"Yes." The back part of my vertebra had been removed to relieve the pressure on my nerves.

"Did your surgeon put it back after?"

"I'm not really sure," I said.

"Who was your surgeon?"

I told her. But I did remember something from the Operative Summary. Dr. Ginsberg had sewn in a Neuro-Patch dural replacement. Was this what she meant by putting it back after? My surgeon did what he thought was the best course of action and who was I to argue?

"He probably threw that piece out," Carmen said. "My surgeon said that was the best thing to do. My surgeon said it's only going to cause problems later, so best to just cut it out and throw it in the garbage. I don't have a plastic replacement. I did the right thing."

What was she talking about? "Huh. That's really interesting," I said.

I wanted to punch myself. This was precisely why I had avoided speaking to other patients: They made me doubt my choices. There had been things I had learned early on—when I thought that education in the form of Internet chat rooms was the key to my recovery—that had put me in a tailspin for days. So I had adjusted, learning only as much about my condition as was necessary to keep me moving forward. I had put my future in Dr. Ginsberg's hands and for my faith he had rewarded me with slow, meticulous work that left me with all my body parts moving and accounted for.

Speaking with Carmen was shaking my faith. I decided never again to compare my surgery and progress to others'.

11

To Pee or Not to Pee

Sometime in October, roughly seven weeks after I was admitted to Lyndhurst, I had my family meeting. Every patient got one, like having your day in court, a formalized day of reckoning. At the meeting was my entire team of practitioners: Dr. Zimcik, Dr. Emm, my PT Amanda, OT Heidi, Lorna (who was the acting nurse in Rumy's absence), two residents, and Rich. The team would present the fruits of their labor and, together with the fruits of mine, reveal their findings. Based on that shared information, I would be given an approximate discharge date.

When I entered the room, everyone had big smiles for me, which made me nervous. What could they possibly tell me about my progress that I didn't already know? Who better than me knew how I was doing?

We went around the table.

Amanda: "Ruth is getting a much better sense of where her feet are."

Lorna: "Rumy says Ruth no longer requires pain meds outside of Tylenol."

Dr. Zimcik: "Bladder premonition shows signs of improvement."

After each positive report, I felt an uptick of giddiness. I became the clown in the room; that patient who gave the team hope, reminded them why they got into the care business in the first place, made them laugh and look at each other as if to say: "See? I told you! She has the *best* attitude!"

I was then given two pieces of news: My tentative discharge date was set for November 8 and also, to my great surprise, I was awarded a one-day pass home for Thanksgiving. I hadn't been home since August. I looked at Rich. My faith in the goodness of the universe was fully restored. This was the best, the happiest, the most unexpected surprise I'd had in ages and the joy that came with that surprise lasted a full eight seconds before Dr. Zimcik interrupted.

"Great! So let's discuss what's next. We think you should bring your IC kit home with you."

I couldn't believe this was coming from Dr. Zimcik, my *friend*. To say I felt betrayed by her is not being too dramatic. She knew how hard I had been working to get my bladder back in good working order. She knew me well enough to know that taking my IC home with me would only mean conceding defeat.

I took a deep breath. I had cried every single day since my surgery, but this was no time for tears. I made eye contact with everyone in the room.

"I am not going home with an IC."

Everyone was still smiling, leftovers from the last little joke I must have told.

"That's just in case," someone—a doctor or a nurse or a resident, maybe even Rich—said.

"I'm *not* going home with an IC," I repeated. "Oh, I'm going *home*, all right, just *not* with an IC."

I was small, I was funny, I shared all my chocolates and flowers with the nursing staff, I played Michael Jackson loudly in my room, I told good stories and listened to sad stories. I could tell I was one of those patients they talked about on their coffee breaks. I knew some of them had looked me up on the Internet Movie Database (IMDb) and then possibly went home and told their children that they were caring for an actress who was in this show or that show. I could feel myself being assessed with fresh eyes. But I didn't care. I was not going home with an IC. I abruptly wheeled out of the room. The meeting was over.

When I was little, the story goes that my grandmother bought me a beautiful pair of flowered underpants. She put them on my bed and told me that I was not allowed to wear them until I learned to use the washroom on my own. At that point in my life, I had yet to speak a single word, which made my father wring his hands with worry. He begged my mother to take me to the doctor, but she refused.

"She understands everything. She'll talk when she's ready."

The day my grandmother presented her bribe, I promptly left my room where my new pair of underwear lay fanned across my bedspread like a cotton gusset bouquet. I went straight to my mother.

"Take these diapers off. Now." I was ready to talk.

After my family meeting that day at Lyndhurst, I felt as fierce and determined as my two-year-old self. From then on, at the slightest flurry of nerve activity, I wheeled myself to the washroom. I would transfer myself to the toilet. Then I would wait, and wait, and wait. *It's fine*, I told myself. *No rush. You can sit here all day.* Even though I was lucky enough to be in a private room, the word *private* was open for interpretation. I always slid the bathroom door shut, but that didn't mean the nurses wouldn't walk in unannounced. The first time this happened I screamed, "Hey!"

The nurse laughed. "Oh, you're shy?"

"Not really," I said. "Just kind of don't want company in the bathroom."

She hooted, then turned on the tap. "Listen to the sound of the water and meditate."

Another nurse advised me to "get angry" in order to get things moving. Yet another suggested that I tap my stomach to wake my sleeping bladder. I tried everything they said. My attempts were often frustrating, tear-inducing, fruitless, until I started to listen more carefully to the new signals my nerves were sending, and in turn my body started to respond. It was like overhearing a secret and then acting on the information before someone—or something, like my IC—did it first. I praised my bladder as though it were my child. *Good bladder. You've got this!* I hugged my belly and whispered to it in a quiet voice. Eventually, the number of times I had to return to my room for an IC was outnumbered by the legitimate bathroom trips I initiated on my own. The nurses were cautiously encouraging; I could tell they didn't want me to get ahead of myself. Every day it was milligram this and milliliter that. Although I still cooked based on the imperial system, and calculated my height in feet and inches and my weight in pounds, it was important for me to nail the metric system down in order to understand what dosage of which drug I was taking and, of even greater importance, how much I had to pee to keep that snake-like tube away from my hoo-ha.

It turns out the answer lay not in how much I peed, but in how much I didn't.

"Talk to me like I'm a child," I said to Juliette, my rock 'n' roll French nurse. "Exactly what are you measuring?"

"No matter 'ow much you pee, there is always some urine that remains in your bladder, *oui*? There is both an acceptable and an unacceptable amount."

"Which is?"

"If I do a bladder scan after you pee and there is less than one hundred mils remaining, you will not need an IC."

"I can do that!"

"Wait, madame. You need a reading of one hundred mils or less, three times in a row," she clarified.

"How about three times over the course of a week?"

"In a row."

"How about twice, but then there's a blip, say, but then the *next* time the reading is under one hundred?"

"Three times *in a row*."

Until that point, I hadn't fully accepted exactly how crucial my nerves were to every single function in my body. My whole life, I had put muscles and bones at center stage. I never gave much thought to my nerves, even as they plugged away behind the scenes, making only brief but dramatic appearances before exams, big auditions, and saying "I love you" for the first time to Rich.

Now I listened to my nerves and waited, after two perfect bladder scans, for that crucial third time *in a row* to pee.

I felt it!

I rolled quickly to the bathroom, peed, rolled quickly back to bed, pulled my leggings down below my belly button, rang for a nurse before my bladder filled up again, and waited impatiently for a scan.

Juliette answered the call. She rolled the scanner over my stomach as I watched. Her face betrayed nothing.

"FOR GOD'S SAKE, WHAT DOES IT SAY?"

She looked at the scanner and sighed dramatically before very slowly turning the screen my way.

Less than 100 mils! The magic number!

I burst into tears.

"You are 'appy, uh?"

I would never have to look at that clear rubber tube of evil again.

12

A Taste of Home

One Wednesday morning in October I woke up crying, but it wasn't for the same old reasons. Amanda and Heidi had informed me that they needed to do an analysis of my house before I was fully cleared to go home that weekend on my official Thanksgiving day-pass. I would accompany them on their visit. It would be for a couple of hours only, but still—home.

We piled into the taxi, my wheelchair disassembled and tossed into the trunk. I sat with my face pressed against the window, weeping soundlessly, completely overwhelmed by what lay ahead. Amanda and Heidi didn't even try to engage me. They whispered quietly to each other like they were in church. They were armed with notepads, pens, pencils, and measuring tapes. They needed to make sure my home would be a hospitable environment for someone in a wheelchair. I felt like a harvested vital organ. Was it possible that my own house would reject me?

When we pulled onto my street, giant sobs burst from me, all manner of honking and gasping and nose-blowing that was wildly out of proportion to the actual event, which was a simple right-hand turn into my driveway. Amanda and Heidi looked alarmed.

Lyndhurst felt as far away as Iceland when in fact it was less than fifteen minutes from my house.

Rich was on the porch waiting for us. He remembered perfectly how to unfold my chair, working in his assured and confident way, and then he helped me out of the car. I cursed our "modern aesthetic," which prevented us from getting a railing for our front steps because we thought it wouldn't look cool. I saw Heidi jot something down in her notebook. With or without a railing, I had to get up the stairs—the first hurdle between me and my house.

"Do you remember how to do this?" Rich asked, holding his hands out.

"I'm scared."

"I've got you."

Rich held me close. I tried to remember what I had been taught about climbing stairs; how to step up and down and over and around things, and how to balance against my partner so that we moved in sync, with me leaching just enough of my partner's strength to keep myself upright.

It wasn't long before we had an audience. Our neighbor across the street leaned on his rake and waved an uncertain hello. People on the sidewalk, supportive strangers, slowed to watch. Then my older sister, Karen, appeared, walking her dog. She lives right behind us and of course she knew, as my whole family did, that I was coming home that day, but she couldn't possibly have known how auspicious her timing would be.

"Ruthie," she called, but didn't come closer as I struggled up the stairs with Rich's help. Even her yappy dog stopped yapping so he could stare. I wanted to say something, but I was capable of only two things: crying and gripping Rich's arms.

Our stairs were uneven, the distance between one step and the next changing each time. It was Amanda who noticed this discrepancy and called out a warning. She and Heidi hovered over me. Amanda was watching as nervously and excitedly as I had when Joey took his first steps. Would she be more proud of me for getting myself up the stairs or for teaching me how to do it? Who cares? We were all wrapped in the same hug of victory when I made it to the top.

Amanda and Heidi lingered a few steps behind me when Rich opened the door.

"You're home, babe."

I walked in. The house was bursting with color. The red carpet made the whole dining room glow pink. The blue glass wall behind our stove sparkled. The windows at the back of the house framed a few quivering yellow leaves still hanging on to their branches. The sun highlighted the tiny pinpoints of dust spinning in the air. I wanted to touch everything, kiss everything, *clean* everything. *My kingdom*, I thought, *for a Swiffer, a DustBuster, and some wet paper towel.* I wanted to shake out the rugs— something I had never done before in my life. I wanted to touch every surface and say: *mine mine mine.* But instead, I settled for doing what I did best: drinking in as much as my eyes could hold and then bawling it all back out.

Heidi and Amanda left Rich and me in the front hall.

"Can we go upstairs, Richie?" I asked. "I need to see our room."

We danced slowly up the steps; I counted each one as we went—fifteen in all. At the top, I made good use of our banister. The hardwood floor was slippery, inspiring me to drag myself along rather than load my feet down with the still mystifying concept of lifting and landing.

Rich helped me onto our bed, which was so high up that my feet dangled when I sat on the edge. I lowered myself onto my back, not caring how much it hurt, and then turned my head to the side.

"I love our bed so much!" I cried.

Rich hopped up beside me and I spoke directly into his armpit. "So *much*!" I repeated. We held each other and didn't let go, even when Heidi and Amanda came into our room without knocking—just like we were still at Lyndhurst. I had been so lonely without Rich and my kids, so lonely without my things. I missed my crisp white duvet and my puffy pillows. I missed all my books and Rich's poker manuals. I missed my overstuffed bedside table drawers and my dumb Ikea lamps that always tipped over. I missed Henry's warm body stumbling into our room before school and wedging between us. I closed my eyes. I didn't have the strength to walk around and peek inside every room. I already knew what I would find in Joey's room—a tangle of clothes on the floor and one inverted sock—the other sock would surely be in the bathroom where he always left it after his shower, specifically to make me crazy. I felt an almost hysterical greediness. I didn't want to make do anymore with the dribs and drabs of home that I had at Lyndhurst. I wanted *all* of it back.

But I wouldn't have to miss any of it for much longer. My twenty-four-hour day pass was for that very weekend, three days away. Everything was going to be perfect.

●

"I'm going to make lunch."

"No, you're not."

"Yes, I am."

"Ru, you need to rest. That's what Dr. Zimcik explicitly told you. She said you have to take it easy, that you can't do too much, that—"

"I know what she said. I'm making lunch."

Lunch was all I could think about once Rich and the kids picked me up at Lyndhurst to bring me home for the day. We stopped at the little produce store around the corner. I had no idea what we had in the fridge, but I had a pretty good idea what we didn't. I wrote out a quick list in the car: avocado, cherry tomatoes, red peppers, corn, feta cheese, tuna—all the things I would need for a big, fat salad. Ah—and cheddar cheese! I would make grilled cheese sandwiches for the kids. We would all sit around the table and laugh and talk over one another, just like a reality TV family.

Rich helped me inside the house, just as we had practiced, and got me settled into my favorite chair by the fire. He unpacked the groceries and started preparing lunch. I insisted, again, that he let me make it. My instinct was to jump up and run over if he so much as touched my tomatoes. The fact that I couldn't do either didn't stop me from making a threatening move forward. With a heavy sigh, he helped me into the kitchen where I got to work.

I used everything within reach—and, miraculously, everything *was* within reach—to pull myself up. I had only to swivel and pivot and take just one step here or there without letting go of the kitchen island in order to prepare lunch. Amanda and Heidi were thrilled with the layout of the house and had shown me how effectively I could get around just by using the walls and countertops as my touchstones.

I had been craving something fresh, something made with my own hands, something with *color*. The closest I'd come to anything resembling vegetables, other than the sad broccoli served most nights at Lyndhurst, were the dried green edamame pods I got inside my Asian cracker mix, the snack with which my mother kept me well supplied. I could feel Rich's worry and agitation while I busied myself. I ignored his pleas for me to sit down.

The boys were right behind me on their computers in the sunroom, as if it was any other day, as if everything was totally normal.

"Mom," I heard Henry say. "Mom."

I turned around.

"Mom," he said again, and there were tears in his eyes. "I can't believe it."

"I know, Hank. Come here."

He came to me and we hugged standing up. I shoved my nose in his hair like he was a baby again, only his head didn't smell like a baby's—it smelled like cheese.

It wasn't until we sat down for lunch that I realized I had been standing for several minutes. My walker was always right behind me in case I needed a rest, and Rich's eyes were practically glued to me, on the lookout for any treacherous signs of sway from which he might have to rescue me, and yes, I had slid from spot to spot in the kitchen while gripping the countertops instead of actually lifting my feet, but it all counted, didn't it? I would be sure to report my progress to Amanda on Monday. Maybe I was ready for the next step.

For the rest of the day, I made myself ostentatiously comfortable. I stretched my legs out luxuriantly on the ottoman and angled my feet toward the fire. The heat soothed every nerve in my body. I rubbed my hand over my legs and noticed, quite by accident, that a small patch on my right thigh had quietly returned to its former self. Being home was already working its magic.

The pressure was off my boys to stay close, something they tried to do when they came to visit at Lyndhurst. At home, they didn't have to be right there with me—it seemed to be enough to know that I was in the house. When I heard a toilet flush upstairs, I was happy. When the boys left their dishes all over the place, I shrugged. I was floating inside a bubble where pain and discomfort, no matter how sharp, could not prick my happiness. I was just about as relaxed as I could be, right up until dinner.

I don't remember how the fight began or who started it, only that without warning Rich and I were scrapping with each other. He was going back and forth from the table, clearing the dishes and piling plates up in the sink without rinsing them first. Couldn't he see he was doing everything wrong? And where were the kids? Why did they just disappear without helping? Why weren't they fawning all over me, tripping over each other to tell me stories and to hug and kiss me? And why was there no music playing? Had Joey been practicing the piano *at all* since I'd been gone? And what was this I heard about him getting a lousy mark on his science test? Was nobody making sure that the kids were doing their homework after school? And Jesus Christ, when was the last time somebody actually took a wet sponge and wiped down the goddamn table?

Rich valiantly tried to avoid the fight. "We're doing the best we can, Ru."

I leaned into my tirade, until Rich shook his head and walked away.

"That's not fair!" I said. "You can't just leave me stranded here. I'm mad and I want to walk away too but I can't just *pop* up and *stomp* out of the room. *FUCK!*"

Rich's body language changed as he came back to get me. He bent forward and brought his hands under my elbows, the same way he does when he's helping his ninety-seven-year-old mother into the car. Over the years, I have often thought that I could take a lesson from him on how to treat people with respect and kindness.

My stomach hissed and rumbled ominously. When it turned on like that, I couldn't concentrate. In my quest to chase down the origin of the signals my nervous system was sending, I thought it was necessary to act on every one my body received. Consequently, I would find myself rolling to the bathroom at the tiniest inkling of a warning that something worthwhile might happen. My body cried wolf ten, twenty, thirty times a day. But standing in my kitchen, far from the intensity of Lyndhurst, I finally wised up and saw my body for what it was—just a big bag of tricks that loved to fool me, loved to make me think that something *momentous* was about to take place just so it could call me out for the sucker I was. Well, I had no time for its dramatic rumblings that led nowhere.

Rich helped me up. I slid the three or four steps it took to get to the kitchen island. I grabbed the edges and looked up at him, but just then, the noise from my stomach increased. I opened my mouth to alert Rich to my potential need to get to the bathroom, when out came the longest, rollingest, loudest, most *shofar*-blowing, bloat-reducing fart. Rich and I listened in awe. It went on long enough for me to remember all kinds of things, like the movement teacher I had in theater school who made all the students lie on the floor and imagine breathing in through their anuses and out through their eyes, which prompted my friend Fli to whisper: *It would probably be easier if we reversed that.* I thought about how every couple has its own rules, some as obvious as not having an affair to as idiosyncratic as not eating apples in bed. Our rule was quaintly civilized: no tooting in front of each other. Amazingly, after so many years together, we had managed to honor this rule, even when I was in the hospital. But there it was, the last bit of mystery between my beloved husband and me, gone. I stood shakily before him: a lame, angry, farty little wife. It was hard for either of us to stay mad after that.

I watched Rich do all the dishes and I didn't complain once.

13

Walkabout

Color was a big deal at Lyndhurst, mostly for the lack of it. Men often wore flannel pajama bottoms to their physio appointments, and women defaulted to the drabbest colors in their wardrobes. Even I had edited my clothing down to only those pieces that were variants on concrete: sand, mushroom, pewter, black. My fashion sense was in mourning for the old me. When my friend Liza visited one afternoon, she defied rather than deferred to my drab environment. She arrived in an outfit that made her look as dazzling as a peacock in a field of goats. She wore a pair of tall boots and a multicolored wrap over skinny jeans. It was like having a front row seat at Mardi Gras.

"It's hard to imagine being interested in shopping ever again," I told her. "My legs and bum routinely reject whatever I put on them. It's *them*, and not the mirror, that reigns supreme over all my fashion choices, little dictators. Ergo, these." I pointed. My legs could only withstand the softest and stretchiest of fabrics, which meant leggings. Every. Single. Day.

"That'll change," she said. "Eventually, there will be enough room to bring those things you love back into your life."

"Maybe," I said. "I miss being shallow."

Somehow, I had conferred a kind of depth to people in wheelchairs, as if by their very disability they carried something preternaturally *known*, something regular bipeds, with their easily moving body parts, couldn't possibly understand. I was convinced that my thoughts were fuller, more intense than they were before the surgery. It looked like my friends shared my thinking, given how stressed out they became when they caught themselves complaining. They would abruptly stop talking, midsentence, and look at me with shame or horror. "I can't believe what I'm complaining about when you're going through *this.*"

This was indicated with one upturned hand, as if my world had shrunk to the size of their palm. But the truth was, I loved hearing the griping because it meant that for a moment they had forgotten my woes, which gave me permission to do the same.

One day, my friend Michael came to visit me. This was the same friend who was convinced that his eye twitches meant he had ALS. I was in the kitchenette beside the nurse's station filling up my water jug when I caught him wandering the halls, already sweaty, looking for my room. When I wheeled over to him, he stopped dead in his tracks.

"It's okay, Michael, it's okay. Here—let's go to my room." I kept up a one-sided dialogue filled with chipper exclamations: *Did you bring me lunch? Ooh, what's that? Sushi—just what I was hoping for. Let's eat!*

Once Michael's color brightened and we squeaked open all the Styrofoam containers, he returned to his chatty self. I wanted to hear everything that was going on in his life.

"The news isn't great," he said, before launching into his most pressing concerns. "It feels as if there are troubles lurking around every corner."

"Oh, my friend," I said. I was listening to every word, but I was also impatient to show him my fantastic leg-crossing trick. He hadn't even noticed that I was practicing while he spoke, which was perfect. I was going to blow his mind!

"Anyway," he continued, just as I lost track of my left foot. I ducked down to see if it was under my footrest. "The point is, I have just been so un*lucky*."

My eyes bulged as if I had been hit in the head with a frying pan. *Unlucky?* I wanted to yell. *Are you fucking kidding me?!*

I had a choice: I could cry or I could laugh or I could box his ears. I needed a moment to think.

"I have to find my foot," I said. "I know it's here somewhere."

Michael looked horrified.

Maybe this was my fault, I thought. Maybe I made the whole wheelchair thing look easy, like just another bothersome stage in the aging process. Maybe by taking extra care to make sure everyone else was comfortable in my strange surroundings, I gave the impression I wasn't having a hard time.

"Found it!" I said. I put my foot back on the footrest. "Gotta be vigilant or my feet might just leave without me, know what I'm saying?"

But of course, he didn't know what I was saying. No one did.

He shook his head, concern—for himself and for me—etched in the lines on his face. I didn't laugh or cry or throw a fit. Instead, I gave Michael's arm an affectionate squeeze. We were all struggling.

•

At home on my second day pass, I was in our powder room next to the kitchen, a room so narrow you can barely extend your arms all the way out. While in there, it occurred to me that there were enough things for me to grab—the sink, the towel rack, the glass shelf over the toilet—should I decide to take a few tentative steps on my own. Amanda discouraged this kind of rogue behavior, but she did so halfheartedly. She knew the key to my progress was testing my limits. My daily practice by the picnic table was a means to an end, not an end in itself. All the most significant decisions I had made in life took place this way: in a small moment, without consultation, quickly. I let go of the sink and shuffle-walked to the door with my hands in the air as if a cop had hollered *freeze!* I turned the door handle, then let go instantly; I didn't want to depend on its stability for even one second longer than I had to. There was nothing and no one behind me to catch me if I fell. In the door frame, I balanced, swayed. I was, literally, freestanding.

"Richie," I called. "Rich!"

"Do you need me?" he called back.

"Come!"

I blinked and he was standing right in front of me, unsure if what he was seeing was real.

"Don't touch me," I said. "Just hold your arms out."

I started my toddler-of-Frankenstein walk out of the powder room, my eyes locked on the third button of his shirt. He took tiny steps backward as I took tiny steps forward.

"Boys! Come here!" Rich called. They got off their computers faster than I'd ever seen them do before or since. Rich snapped his fingers. "Joey!"

In a flash Joey was behind me; Rich stayed in front. Henry, who was practically in tears, could do little more than hang on to the kitchen counter, watching in disbelief.

I was breathing hard, staccato breaths that threatened to turn into full-on hyperventilating.

"Relax," Rich instructed.

I walked fifteen steps, beating Joey's first baby steps by a measure of four. Then, just as my son had done so many years ago, I collapsed into the waiting arms of my family.

•

Galvanized by the steps I had taken at home, Amanda added the treadmill to our daily physio appointments. Victor was my designated people-walker. He was a much-loved, much-needed presence at Lyndhurst, filling in all the gaps that fell out of other staffers' jurisdictions. He helped move patients in and out of gym apparatus, walked alongside them as they got used to their walking sticks, was always squatting down to fix or adjust something—a wheel, a shoelace, an ankle. He was a handyman for the animate and inanimate alike.

I couldn't walk on the treadmill unassisted, which meant I had to wear the harness that hung from the ceiling. It looked like a fetishistic diaper. At the beginning of my stay at Lyndhurst, I would watch people get holstered into that thing and feel a jealousy fiercer than anything I'd ever known. But when my turn came to finally use it, I was gripped by fear. It was as if the few steps I had taken at home had never happened. I couldn't figure out what I was supposed to do with the two long appendages hanging from my hips. Victor stood behind me, holding the back of the belt that was attached to the holster like a leash. He called out instructions to me as I slowly walked: *Squeeze your glutes, activate your bum, lift the knee, roll your foot, heel* then *toe, heel* then *toe.* How could I activate my bum muscles when I couldn't even feel them? Since I couldn't differentiate between my toe and my heel, how on earth was I supposed to figure out which one came first? My left leg wanted to be someplace else, while my right leg tried hard to stay the course. I always thought my legs were such good friends, but it turns out they were just two folks married to the same body, living together but apart. The right sleeve of my cardigan had grown damp from where I kept wiping my blurry eyes and my runny nose. Victor was trying not to notice that I was falling apart.

"Can I please have a Kleenex, Victor?"

He pulled two tissues from the box at the far side of the room and returned to me. I could see him thinking: *If* I *don't become too reactive then* Ruth *won't become too reactive.* I took the Kleenex and honked and wiped and sighed and, in time, got it together. His grace under pressure, in the face of a crying woman wearing a giant diaper, actually helped calm me down. Victor unhooked me in various spots around my body. I was done for the day.

"Sorry about my blubbering," I said.

"No need to apologize," he said. "See you tomorrow—same place, same time."

Everything was homework. Dancing in my room, while fun, was homework. Learning how to keep time, how to force my feet to move in appropriate ways, was homework. I would close my eyes and tell my feet to turn this way and that and then open my eyes to make sure they were doing it right. Always, my right foot was the A student, while my left foot was a spaced-out stoner. I would lay a napkin on the floor and try to grab it with my toes with the understanding that gripping was one of the key components of walking. This was when the spasticity in my toes was most evident. Each toe felt like the size of a balloon. Scrunching them, while doable, still didn't make sense to my brain. I slid one foot up and down my calf and then again on the other side, just like my cousin Joel told me to do, every night. I put my feet through their paces, every single day, and then hoped that sleep would do the rest: Commit the work to memory, reset my will, keep the tears at bay.

In the morning, I went straight from physio to the treadmill where Victor was waiting to push my wheelchair up the ramp and strap me inside the diaper. I didn't think about what I looked like—I didn't care. I also stopped caring if my legs went all jelly-like and lost stride or my ankles turned over when my rhythm was off.

"I'm fine," I'd call back to Victor. "I'll get it. Let's just keep going."

"You got it, boss." He held on to the leash attached to my holster.

I couldn't help thinking: *I'm Victor's bitch.*

"How many minutes have I gone?" I called.

"Six or so. Can you make it to ten?"

"Maybe."

Sometimes I could only get to eight, sometimes ten, on a bad day, five. I accepted these numbers, dropped them into the void, and then shook it off. There was always tomorrow and the day after that and the day after that.

"Ruth," Victor said one afternoon, after slowing the treadmill to a halt.

"What's the matter? Why did we stop? Was I messing up?"

"You went twelve minutes."

"I did? I thought we were only going to go ten."

"Well, you went twelve."

"Holy shit."

"I think it's time to move on."

I knew what he meant. I was already crying. "You think I'm ready for the sticks."

"I do."

"Holy holy shit. Get me out of this thing."

Two walking sticks with tiny rubber feet on the bottom.

I practiced going round and round the PT room with Amanda by my side. I could tell from the stiffness in her arms that she was holding back from holding on to me. I kept my back as straight as possible, my head held high. I aimed for dignified but had to settle for Monty Python.

My balance was wonky and unpredictable. I still had the sense my feet were hovering above the ground rather than touching it, but I tried to play it cool, tried not to stare at them too much as if staring might give them performance anxiety. Once I had practiced several times with Amanda, I was cleared to do it without supervision.

Alone in my room, I removed my shoes and placed them neatly to the side of my chair, like I was entering a Japanese teahouse—quietly, simply, elegantly. Then I planted my feet and scrutinized them. I memorized their position on the floor and gathered as much sensory information as I could. I hoisted myself up using my sticks as leverage. I looked left and right, as if a car might suddenly vroom out of my tiny closet. Then, almost like any other regular biped, I walked out of my room.

Several nights into this new routine, I had to make my way past two senior wheelies in the TV lounge watching *Dancing with the Stars*. The ladies' smiling profiles told me how much they were enjoying the show. They didn't look at me, not even during commercial breaks. I was a little disheartened by this, as I had grown dependent on my daily dose of praise, whether it came from my apple supplier, Neville, or my new best friend, Dr. Zimcik, or my comrade in arms, Rei. In return, I paid it forward, tossing out motivational words whenever it looked like a patient could use them. But I was barking up the wrong ladies if I thought I could eke a compliment out of either of them. After three walkabouts, I finally gave up when I realized, with some embarrassment, that not every patient grew excited by the prospect of *another* patient's newfound ability to walk. I went to the nurses' station. Lorna, a big nurse with brown, bushy hair, was there. She was loading pills into little pleated paper cups.

"Watch me, Lorna?"

She stopped counting her pills.

"Do I look lame?"

"No."

"Do I look gimpy?"

"No."

"Do I look . . . pretty?"

"Yes."

"Thank you," I said.

We looked at each other. Her blue eyes exactly matched her blue scrubs.

"Well, it's true," she added.

"Anyway," I said. "Thanks."

14

Working Girls

There were two TV shows I couldn't stop watching—shows that for different reasons were the worst possible programs a person living in a hospital could watch. The first worst was *The Big C*, with a premise that revolved around the main character secretly having cancer—but it was funny! As a result, many nights before I fell asleep, I would make a mental note to discuss my latest ailments with Dr. Zimcik, since I was pretty sure I also had cancer. Sometimes I thought it was ovarian, other times bowel, often kidney.

And then there was *Friday Night Lights*—a show I should have stopped watching after the first episode, when the star quarterback of the series, after one brutal hit in his first football game of the season, ends up paralyzed from the waist down. In the hospital scenes, I noticed that the set was dressed with, among other things, the exact same tray table that I used every day. I became fascinated with the quarterback's journey. I watched, pressing my hand tightly to my chest, as he moved through the five stages of grief and I cried when he arrived at the same sets of challenges that I had: the blisters on my hands from pushing the wheels of my chair, the switch to batting gloves, the frustration of transferring from the wheelchair to anywhere else. I had never been so invested in a TV character—including the ones that I had played. I searched for false notes in his performance but couldn't find them. I watched, with my fingers over my eyes, as he attempted to have sex with his girlfriend, still unsure what exactly he was working with. And when he miraculously made another girlfriend pregnant, I wept happy tears for both of them, but also sad tears for myself, for the lost narrative in my life that would have catapulted my story into movie magic. What if I *had* become pregnant after Rich and I had sex in the hospital? What would that have looked like for someone in the midst of relearning how to walk, let alone in her late forties? But what I was also experiencing was a lost sense of self. Although I wasn't feeling like much of a wife or a mother, I knew those parts of my life would eventually bounce back, but my career? I wasn't so sure.

One night, after finishing an episode of *The Big C* and then having a Big Cry, I decided to check my IMDb page, where an actor's complete résumé is listed along with her headshots. I found my page easily but my accompanying photo had mysteriously disappeared. In its place was a generic gray and white silhouette. Was this a sign? Was the universe sending me a message? Were my acting days over?

It made me think of a lecture Rich and I had attended. The speaker, a rabbi, had just found out his wife was pregnant when he learned he had cancer. Lying in his hospital bed next to another patient, he was asked why he never prayed to God to spare him, and the rabbi said: *Why should God take the time to spare me over someone else? What makes me so special?* Remembering this brought me back to earth; this wasn't a sign, it was a glitch, and who cared that my picture was gone? It wasn't as if I was acting anymore, anyway.

But how long had my picture been down? Did Jennifer's assistant, in an attempt to divest her of the dead weight on her roster, make the unilateral decision to take it down? Did Jennifer know something I didn't? *Did somebody somewhere know something I didn't?*

I wrote an email to my agent.

Hi Jenn!

I noticed that my headshot is no longer on my IMDb page and it made me very sad because, well, it makes me feel as if I'm disappearing.

So although this could hardly be considered a priority at this stage, can you please ask your assistant to call IMDb headquarters and kindly ask them to put my fucking picture back up?

Thank you so much!
Ruth

I remembered an argument my father and I had had many years earlier, right after I graduated from university. I was getting ready to move out and he wanted to know how I planned on making a living. That part was easy: I would temp and wait tables while looking for a talent agent to represent me.

My father was dubious. "You want to be an actress," he said. I didn't like his tone and looked to my mother for support. Wisely, she let my father and I have it out without running interference (a skill I never quite learned).

"I can't believe I have the kind of father who would stop me from following my dreams!" I shouted.

"I'm not stopping you. I just think your talents would be better served elsewhere."

I snorted. "Doing what? I have a degree in English Lit. I am qualified to do approximately nothing."

"I happen to think you'd be a very good writer."

I was thrown. He had never mentioned this before—this was even more bonkers than wanting to be an actress. "You really think I'd make more money as a *writer*?"

Despite his reservations, my father didn't stand in my way—in fact, once I made it clear that I was going to do exactly what I set out to do, he became my champion. At forty-seven, with a healthy acting career behind me, I felt for the first time as if I might have wrung out as much from my career as I could. Maybe it was time to try something new. The one thing that I had been doing every single day—besides crying, taking pills, and talking about sex— was writing. I had been keeping meticulous notes for months, ever since my feet began tingling. It had become a habit.

I took out my notebooks then, curious to revisit the past. I flipped to a random page—sometime in April, six months earlier. At that point the doctors were baffled by my symptoms. My eyes scanned the page and landed on one sentence.

"I think I have a tumor."

I didn't tell Rich or the doctors, not my friends or my family. In fact, I had no memory of writing that line. Such was the power of my denial and fear that when I was finally diagnosed, I was as shocked as everyone else.

I turned out my lights. I wasn't preoccupied with my IMDb page or my acting career or my notebooks anymore. All I could think was: *What would my life look like now if I had just said something then?*

•

Sometime around mid-October, three things happened.

First, while I was on my nightly walk around the halls of unit

2B, I stopped Rumy to ask her what she thought of my fancy footwork.

"Don't you think I look good?" I asked, walking and then coming to an unsteady halt like a slightly drunk army sergeant.

"I can tell that you can't feel your feet."

This was like being told by a director, in front of the entire cast and crew, that she knew I was faking it.

"Anyway," I said, and I hobbled away.

I completed my rounds of the unit, slapping the ground with my seal flipper feet. I didn't know then that Rumy's honesty, as much as it stung, would turn out to be the best thing she could have said.

The second event happened when my agent told me that *Degrassi* wanted to book me for an upcoming episode. They were aware of my situation and had been understanding and patient. Now they wanted me back. But how? I wasn't ready. I couldn't walk—not well, anyhow. Working was impossible. I waited as long as I could and then said no.

It was the third event, however, that stirred up the most drama: A movie star sent me flowers.

At the beginning of my Lyndhurst stay, the movie star and his famous director wife sent me a stunning bouquet of pink roses. All the nurses clamored around to sniff them, chirping when they saw the signed names on the card. Rich was proud to know that such a famous client of his had been so thoughtful, and I agreed, even though my past feelings about this client and his famous director wife differed somewhat. Rich enjoyed this couple on a pure "they're so talented *and* so nice" level, while I enjoyed them on more of an anthropological level. I watched him like I might watch the chimpanzees at the zoo. I liked the way his hands moved and the way his eyes darted over to his wife after she said something cute and how the famous director's eyes darted back at him and they both laughed, right on cue. They seemed to not need anybody else to make them happy, which was both lovely and off-putting and why sometimes I drank a little too much when I was with them.

The last dinner we had had together, I wore a short black dress and my favorite gray heels. After dinner, Rich put his hand on my back and helped guide me out of the restaurant. My feet wouldn't stop wobbling. It was August, soon after our trip to Peru but before I knew I had a tumor. Wearing heels (and downing a vodka martini with a red wine chaser) was my way of saying there was nothing wrong with me.

Once I was at Lyndhurst, I felt so open to the world and its multiple kindnesses. Rich was right: The movie star and his director wife were among the nicest famous people I had ever met, and his roses were beautiful. I sent the movie star a heartfelt thank-you note. A few weeks later, the second bouquet arrived.

"What's this?" I asked the nurse who delivered them.

The flowers were red. I hate red flowers.

"Do you want me to take the wrapping off?"

"No, thank you," I said. "Can I see the card, please?"

I was lying in bed, before dinner, something I swore I would never do. It had been a bad day. I was a miserable, vibrating, buzzing, burning, static-electric lady of leisure—a sad, lonely woman who spent huge swaths of her day in bed trying to fart.

The nurse passed me the card.

Wishing you a speedy recovery. Love, Movie Star and Famous Director.

Anger suddenly propelled me out of bed. I transferred into my wheelchair and put the fat box of horrible red flowers onto my lap and wheeled over to the nurse's station.

"Take them, just take them," I said to the nurse there.

"But they're so pretty! Why don't you want to keep them?"

"I just don't."

I wheeled back to my room before she could say anything else. I leaned my elbows on my stupid buzzing legs and pushed my palms into my stupid graying hair. Did the movie star completely forget that he'd already sent me flowers with the *exact* same card and the *exact* same words? Did he think I just sat in my room all day waiting for moments like this to feel *grateful* for his kindnesses? Did he think I didn't have any *friends*, for fuck's sake? I finished an entire bag of jujubes while my heart thumped restlessly.

I always believed that a heavy dose of charm and confidence would take me wherever I wanted to go, no matter the situation. But stripped of the ability to stride in and out of a room, to make decisions on my feet, to take corners without hesitation, I was lost. It seemed that all the emotional and psychological strength I had built up over the years had somehow pooled in my legs, and without them, I was making false moves, inexplicable moves, wrong moves. I was all over the place and yet moving nowhere at all. In the absence of knowing for sure, I made up what others thought of me, and the stories I told myself weren't particularly nice. I had decided that the movie star saw me as a sad, incapable, pathetic woman in need of gifts. And that's when I realized: *Oh, for fuck's sake. They're* JUST FLOWERS.

I took a deep breath, opened my computer, and tapped out a thank-you note. It didn't say much, but it was one of the most heartfelt I have ever sent.

Really, I wrote. *Thank you.*

•

It felt like overnight the intensity of my care dropped from a Code Blue to a Code She Can Wait. The dynamic with those around me, mostly my nurses, changed. Because I was more open to their preoccupations, my room became a kind of confessional. I loved my nurses with their finely tuned observational skills and tactfulness. My more relaxed body language must have spoken to them and the words they heard were: *Tell me everything.*

One night nurse was funny and scattered and loved a good laugh. She would stop by my room for last call to drop off my pills, then hang around, fussing over things that didn't need fussing. We mostly talked about our kids and our plans for their futures. Her partner's name came up occasionally, mostly in terms of his being a good father. But one night, she told me that she didn't love him—had never loved him. I nodded sympathetically as she spoke.

"I met someone else, though. Someone from my twins' school." She looked behind her, then lowered her voice. "Someone married."

"Oh?" I said.

"Yes. I love this man so much. One day, I saw his wife eating at McDonald's." She plumped up my pillow and readjusted my call button. "If I had a knife, I would have stabbed her."

I stayed very still.

"I mean it. I really wanted to stab her."

"But you, but you wouldn't, right?"

"You know, I've been thinking about you a lot," she said. "I think you can really benefit from acupuncture."

This sounded like an interesting idea, although coming from possibly a crazy person, I decided not to pursue it.

The following morning, Sonja came in with my pills. She was Russian, just a couple years older than me.

"You look so young," she told me in her Russian accent that seemed to be swiped from Joey's small but hilarious Slavic repertoire. "I not only look older than you, I look like I can be your grandmother!"

Sonja had beautiful blue eyes with heavy bags underneath. Her hair was short, bright red and slicked back behind her ears. She also liked to come to my room and tell me stories about her existentialist children. It was Sonja who took my pulse and told me I wasn't pregnant when I thought that maybe (hoped that maybe, feared that maybe) I was. She held my wrist between her fingers and she said, "My first husband was oh, OH, a great kisser, but not much else good. My second husband—*nyet*. But this one, my third, every department good."

"Lucky lady." I said.

"About you," she said, and paused.

Uh-oh. Was it my turn to share?

"I hear you no longer need touches."

Oh. That.

"This is very good news," she said.

"I probably should still have them, but I stopped it."

"I understand."

"I've got to start figuring that shit out on my own—pun fully intended—don't you think?" I really did want to know what she thought. I talked tough, but I was afraid. What if I was never able to generate a bowel movement again without the use of pills?

"I think it's important that you direct your care. Didn't Rumy tell you that?"

I nodded my head. "Rumy knows everything."

"She is very smart lady."

"She sure is."

Rumy was no longer a primary part of my day, even though she was still considered my primary nurse. I saw her most mornings, but our time together was significantly reduced. By Lyndhurst standards, I had been deemed "independent." I no longer needed someone to turn on the tub for me or wheel me in my commode. I no longer needed touches or help getting dressed or transferring to my bed or washing my back or reaching for my hair dryer. I was moving around so much, it had been days since a nurse had stabbed me in the stomach with the blood thinner Heparin so I wouldn't get a blood clot from insufficient movement. I didn't need someone to give me ICs and, at the end of dinner, I no longer needed a nurse to take my tray to the kitchenette for me. All I seemed to need now was friendly banter and someone to make my bed.

But I missed Rumy, even though I still saw her and we still traded information and stories. She kept me up to date on her son's studies and new cashier job. But my days were filling up in different ways now, ways that didn't include her. I was only a couple of weeks away from my discharge date of November 8. We didn't talk about it, just in case it got pushed for some unforeseen reason, but together we were working toward the same goal—to see me leave. There would be other nurses, but no one like Rumy, my primary sweetheart.

15

These Feet Were Made for Walking

Rich and I were the only people who knew my discharge date.

My dad kept asking. "So dear, have they given you any sense of when you might leave?"

He was the one person I would not tell. I simply couldn't—I knew my dad. He would take all his hats and hang them on that hook. He would buy a pick and stone and start carving the date. He would invest his last dollars in that day and tell everyone they could not lose.

"I'm pretty sure it'll be before Christmas, Dad."

"So they haven't said anything exact yet?"

By "they," I think he meant God.

In the meantime, I was making progress on transitioning out of Lyndhurst. For my next new step, I was to go out for lunch instead of dining in. Sheryl offered to take me first.

"You're not in any kind of a rush today, are you?" I asked, as I made my way to the lobby using both my sticks.

"Not at all!"

"Is your car close?"

"So close!"

"Maybe I'll have a drink at lunch."

"Let's drink!"

Sheryl was more nervous than I was.

Getting to the car was relatively easy, and since we were still on Lyndhurst grounds, I wasn't feeling self-conscious. Once we parked outside the restaurant, however, the world felt full of eyes, all of them trained on me.

"You look so good!" Sheryl said. "It must be so nice to be outside! Just take your time. Be careful not to hit the parking meter! Maybe I should hold your elbow. We're almost there! Am I walking too fast for you? You look so pretty!"

I was hyperaware of every change in the pavement, every crack, every stone, every stray piece of litter. My eyes needed to see what my feet might not be able to detect. I felt shy and embarrassed. I was not nearly as smooth and graceful as I had convinced myself I was while in the cozy, supportive atmosphere of Lyndhurst. I was galumphy and tentative. My coordination lacked rhythm; I was still unsure how much space to leave between each step. Sometimes I forgot it was heel *before* toe. Wearing shoes while walking was now foreign to me. I was used to doing everything barefoot except riding in my wheelchair. With my running shoes on, I was amazed at how many layers there were between my feet and the ground, not to mention how horrible it felt wearing socks.

Once we were settled inside the restaurant and I had run my hand around the chair to discern the edges for my permanently out-to-lunch bum, I plopped down.

"Oh no."

"What?" Sheryl said.

"I need to pee."

The restroom was down a steep flight of stairs. I tried to figure out the best course of action.

"I'll go with you," Sheryl said, already getting out of her seat and slinging both our purses, messenger style, over her shoulders. "There's not enough room for you to use your sticks. Hold my hand."

I let her lead the way. We stopped at the top of the stairs and looked at the long way down. The restaurant owner appeared next to me, carrying a plate of pad Thai.

"This is going to be really hard for you," she said, and then left to deliver her order.

"That was helpful," I said, once she was out of earshot.

"We can do this," Sheryl said. "I'll go down in front of you. Don't fall on me."

"But I might."

"Well, don't!"

I went down side step—like coming down a snowy mountain in skis. When we successfully made it to the bottom, I almost wept with joy. When we made it back to our seats, I started laughing.

"Hey!" I said. "We did it!"

"We did." She took a long gulp of water.

"You're not going to barf, are you?"

"Uh-uh." She pressed her napkin to her forehead. "I'm good."

"That was actually kind of fun!" I said. Another hurdle cleared: being out in the world on my own two feet. "I'm starving!"

●

I was lying in bed thinking about shoes when I heard Dr. Zimcik clicking toward my room.

"Ruth? Can I come in?"

My curtain was closed.

"Of course."

I turned over to greet her.

"What's the matter?" she asked. "You never lie down in the morning."

She was wearing a fitted gray dress, two long beaded necklaces, and pretty, flat black shoes. I wondered if those kinds of shoes might look good on me.

"My husband wanted me to eat one of his muffins," I said. "They're his favorite. Packed with fiber and, I'm pretty sure, sawdust. He's convinced they're the key to turning my digestive system around. I told him they make me nauseous. He told me not to insult his muffins."

She laughed.

"How was your trip to New York? Did you buy those pretty shoes there?"

She had gone only for the weekend, but still, I missed her. She told me where she ate, how late she and her girlfriends slept in, and where she shopped. I told her that I had had an appointment with the Lyndhurst urologist, Dr. Aitch.

"I did something stupid after we finished all the bladder business. I asked him if he thought my numb bum would improve and he said that if, after six months, there had been no change, then I couldn't expect any further changes after that." I shrugged, pretending his words didn't affect me.

"That's not necessarily true," Dr. Zimcik said. "It could very possibly take more than six months to change. It could change over the course of years. Everyone is different."

She stayed with me a long time, long enough for me to start talking about my sex life again. "Do you think that doing Kegel exercises will help stir things up down there?"

"I do," she said. "You're probably doing them right now, aren't you?"

She knew everything. "Yes!" I said.

"So am I," she said, and we both laughed.

"Now," I said, "back to your shoes . . ."

·

As my friend Liza had predicted, my life was slowly opening up to more shallow desires. Although clothes sent shivers of discomfort—quite literally—up and down my spine and along my legs, and under my feet, and over my entire bum, I had no interest in living out the rest of my days in leggings and sneakers. I would start at the bottom and work my way up. First, I needed shoes.

Other than my sneakers, I had nothing even remotely appropriate to put on my new feet. My next weekend pass home, Rich drove us all downtown so I could shop. It was pouring, so he pulled up right next to the shoe store and waited in the car with Joey while Henry went in with me. I was using a walker that day instead of my sticks. The walker was incredibly useful for these kinds of outings, although discouraged for use in the long term. I had to bend down to hold on to the arms, which compromised my posture and made walking unnaturally easy. I also used it to practice deep knee bends. My kids would point out—not unkindly—that I looked like a crazy person when I did this, but it was one of the few times, while out in the real world, that I didn't mind if my actions invited curious stares. *If I was dying*, I hoped my body language said, *do you think I'd waste my time doing deep knee bends?*

Henry scooted ahead so he could hold the door open for me. The sales staff were unfazed by my condition. One salesman approached me and I made an ostentatious deal of how I could wear only a certain type of shoe *at the moment*.

"Trust me," I said, even before he had spoken. "This situation right here is temporary. Completely temporary."

I knew what people were thinking when they saw me: *Both her legs seem fine, she obviously didn't break them, she looks so normal, not horrible looking, she has at least one kid, she probably has a husband, must have had sex a few times, she must have taste because she's shopping here, does she have MS?*

I'm fine I'm fine I'm fine, I wanted to say even though there was something obviously wrong with my feet. I thought about Rumy saying she could tell that I couldn't feel the ground. It was true—I still couldn't, not really. I didn't know how much I was faking, how much of what I was doing was based solely on memory, how much was real. I could feel very clearly the buzzing and static, so the problem wasn't that I *couldn't* feel something—the problem was that I felt *too much*. I learned that the profundity of touch was in how little one needed in order to feel with intensity. This constant jackhammering in the soles of my feet drove away all sense of lightness. What if the loss of touch was connected to my loss of self?

I zeroed in on oxfords because they seemed both fashionable and practical. I opted for color—the brightest I could find. Maybe it was because I was sick of wearing only funereal shades, or maybe it was because I suddenly remembered a neat trick from my days as a young music director at camp. I was a terrible piano player, but it was my job to play the national anthem every morning. I hit a stunning number of wrong notes. While I tried to get my nerves and my fingers under control, I would scream through the dining hall window to the bewildered campers below: *Just keep singing!* Finally, one of the lifers from camp—a man who had seen it all, fixed it all, and was also a brilliant self-taught pianist—told me that when I hit a wrong note, I should hit it *hard*. "The harder you hit it, the more people will think you *meant* to hit it."

I thought about this as I considered my shoe options. My eyes naturally went to the black shoes—*You can never go wrong with black*, I could hear people saying. But it takes real confidence to buy royal blue and cherry-red suede shoes.

"Did you also want to look at the pink?" the salesman asked me.

I looked at him carefully to see if he was being sarcastic or not. Although the pink did look tempting.

"A bit too novelty, don't you think?" I said.

"Maybe a little. I think what you've chosen is perfect."

"I think you're right."

Henry and I went to the front of the store to pay for them.

"What?" Henry asked me.

"What what?"

"You're thinking about something," he said.

"Nothing."

But as I handed the cashier my Visa card, I had already made another decision.

Once back at Lyndhurst, I took a good look around my room. There were no flowers on my windowsill anymore. People had stopped bringing them, stopped sending them, even the movie star. The temporariness of the room had given way to a kind of uneasy lived-in vibe. No one flinched when they came to visit anymore. Friends waltzed into my room without having to be reminded how to get there. My parents knew the names of my nurses. The nurses knew the names of my kids; I knew the names of their kids. Watching me, beside my bed, was my wheelchair. I got out of bed, grabbed hold of my sticks, and, unsteady with anger, shoved my wheelchair into the corner of my room. I couldn't stand to look at it anymore. I wanted to call the wheelchair pound to come haul it away. I suppose I could have left it to fester with the other wheelchairs that lined the hallway outside my door, but there was a part of me, even in my pique, that didn't want to break any rules or get anyone in trouble. I considered looking in the binder I had been given upon admittance—the one that warned against smoking weed on the premises— for guidance, but it was a point of pride that I had never read past the first page. It was tucked into a corner of my windowsill—the spot that Kellan's CPA folder used to have before Jeff tried to rip it in half.

My new shoes had gone home with my family while I had to come back here. The oxfords were like the pretty underwear my grandmother bought for me when I was two. In order for me to wear them, I needed to be an upright citizen, but even then, they had no place at Lyndhurst. The hard work happened in my bare feet. Out in the world, I didn't yet trust myself in anything but my sneakers. I got back into bed and plotted my next move. Everything I needed to get me through those last weeks at Lyndhurst was there with me in my room. Everything I needed, and almost nothing I wanted.

•

At five P.M. on Halloween, my adrenalin surging in a way I hadn't felt in months, I decided to leave. It was getting dark and the wind was picking up, but it wasn't raining. I stopped at the nurses' station to let them know I was heading out for a while and to request my meds before I left. It was three-quarters of a kilometer to Starbucks and back, and I was determined to make the journey no matter how long it took me, which was a hell of a lot longer than I anticipated. This was the first time I had been out at night unaccompanied, the first time I had walked with a purposeful destination in mind and not just around and around the grounds of Lyndhurst.

There was something familiar about this feeling. It didn't take long for me to remember. When I was thirteen, my friend Judy and I routinely skipped Hebrew school after our mothers dropped us off. Never wanting to miss an opportunity to be dramatic, we climbed through the bathroom window, jumped onto the gravel below, and then simply wandered around for the next two hours. We were amazed that we never got caught, but also fantasized about the kind of trouble we would get in if we were. It was an exquisite kind of tension. I didn't confess to my mother until long after I had graduated university and moved out. Those escapes were my first real act of rebellion. After almost thirty-four years, this was my second.

By the time I reached the first stop sign, my legs felt stiff and uncomfortable. I wasn't even halfway to Starbucks and it was now fully dark outside and the wind was cold and relentless. I pressed on. Tiny goblins made some brief showings—a few princesses, a bear, a pumpkin-size child in a lion costume. I had enough energy to move around them but none left over to smile at their cuteness. I made it to Starbucks just as it started to rain, hard little pellets that felt like crushed ice. I was freezing.

With the excitement over, I wondered how I was going to get back to Lyndhurst. The truth was, I was exhausted. Dr. Zimcik had warned me against overdoing it now that I felt galvanized by the use of both my walker and my walking sticks, but I had dismissed her concerns. Now, with no one around to offer the kind of help that I would surely have refused if it were offered me, I realized I *had* overdone it. But I had no choice: I had to get back.

By the time I took up my journey again, the streets were packed with trick-or-treaters. Even without a costume, I felt that no one looked scarier than me. Hovering parents made careful-sure to cede the right of way to me and smile kind, sympathetic smiles as I passed. I was slower than the slowest toddler out there, the tortoise among a bunch of hares. We would all make it to the finish line and, unlike the fable, I would definitely get there last, but my triumph would be so much sweeter than theirs, those smooth-walking toddler fuckers.

The hood on my rain jacket was preposterously oversized. When I pulled it over my head, it fell right down past my eyebrows, meaning I had to tip my head almost all the way back in order to see. With my arms stretched taut as I held on to the walker and my head pitched as far back as it would go, I could have won the prize for best costume: I was Lurch from *The Addams Family*.

When I finally made it back to Lyndhurst, I was soaked through. My legs were buzzing madly, my running shoes were drenched, and the seat of my walker was dripping, but I was as happy as I had been in weeks. Forget best costume. I would gladly accept the prize for best performance by an actor pretending to be her old self.

PART THREE

the road home

16

Walking Papers

The next day, Hurricane Sandy knocked out the power all over Lyndhurst. Going to my windowless bathroom meant sliding the heavy wooden door shut and then sitting on the commode with my tiny black flashlight as my only source of light. Treadmill practice was canceled. I couldn't take a shower because there was no hot water. I thought Lyndhurst would have been immune to a storm that originated so far away, but I was wrong. *What could be stranger*, I thought, *than waking up in a dark hospital with a numb bum, alone, and yet still wondering what Dr. Zimcik will be wearing today?*

The morning was shaping up to be useless anyway, so I decided to watch an already downloaded episode of *Friday Night Lights*. And then Dr. Zimcik walked in, the usual spring in her step strangely missing, wearing a corduroy teal blazer with a white T-shirt underneath and a pair of plaid pants, her only adornment a pimple right beside her mouth. Her hair didn't look right, either; she kept touching it like she knew it didn't.

"How are you today?" I asked. It was the first time I had asked her before she asked me.

"Wanna see my baby in her pumpkin costume?"

She pulled out her phone and showed me a video of her littlest one bobbing around their living room with a pumpkin hat and a big pumpkin body.

"Isn't she so cute?! I mean, she's SO cute!"

I laughed with her and nodded my head in agreement. Her enthusiasm made me love her even more.

"What are you watching?" she asked.

"Just a TV show."

I was embarrassed, watching TV at ten thirty in the morning. I might as well have had rollers in my hair, wearing a threadbare robe, watching *Let's Make A Deal*.

"I only have a few things on my agenda, and I'll let you get back to your show."

"Please don't rush!"

"I want to increase your gabapentin."

"Good idea," I said. I couldn't get the buzzing in my legs and bum under control, and it was driving me crazy.

"Also, I need to check the results of your UTI test."

My bladder infection refused to go away.

"I cannot take one more blasted cranberry pill, Dr. Zimcik. I just can't!"

"I get that, I really do. Also," she said, lowering her voice, "I found you the name of a good acupuncturist. At least, I've *heard* she's good."

Dr. Zimcik was dubious that this was the right route to take, but I had been thinking about it ever since that funny little night nurse had suggested it.

"It's worth a shot," I said. "Honestly, outside of drugs, I'll try anything to get my body to shut up."

I was due to be discharged in a week and I wanted everything in place before I left. I was grateful that Dr. Zimcik understood this.

Less than twenty-four hours later, Rumy walked into my room with a staff member I hadn't met before. I looked at both of them, wondering what was up, but only the new woman looked back at me. Rumy was staring at the floor. The new woman broke the news: I was being moved the next day, to a different unit on a different floor with different nurses, to make room for a new patient.

"I'm not at all happy about this," I said, in a surprisingly calm voice.

"I know," the new woman said. "But there's nothing we can do."

"With all due respect, I'd like to speak to the person above you."

"This has gone all the way to the top," she said, waving a hand above her head.

"Is there someone above you?" I asked.

"The executive director, but—"

"Who is the executive director?"

This new woman and Rumy said her name at the same time.

"Is she in her office now?" I asked.

"I think she's in a meeting."

"Where is her office?"

Rumy told me.

"I'd like her phone number, please."

Rumy wrote it out for me, using the wall as her desk. I don't remember the new woman saying good-bye, but quite suddenly she was gone.

"I'm not happy about this," I repeated to Rumy.

"I know," Rumy said. "Neither am I."

How could this have happened? I wondered. Did I do something wrong? Was my music too loud? Had someone complained about me?

"Apparently, it's someone very sick and they need this room," Rumy said, as if she had read my thoughts.

But why my *room?* I wanted to ask. *Why can't someone* else *be transferred out of* their *room?* Even as I thought this, I was shocked at how territorial I had become about this very temporary space, but over the past two months I had worked hard at making peace with my surroundings. I guess I had been more successful than I thought.

I was trying to figure out what to do when Dr. Zimcik and Dr. Emm arrived.

"We've been talking about this," Dr. Zimcik said, word having traveled to her office quickly, "and we think it's absolutely ridiculous to move you. We all do."

Oh thank God, I thought. *They'll make things right for me.*

"But there's nothing we can do."

There wasn't much more to say after that. I called my friend Sheryl to tell her that Lyndhurst was kicking me to another floor and how upset I was about it.

"Can't you just be discharged earlier?"

This sounded reasonable enough, but I lashed out anyway. "I'm not ready to be discharged earlier! I have more physio to do! I'm not leaving until November eighth and I'm not ready to go before then, thank you very much!"

"But that's only seven days away, Ruth," Sheryl said.

I didn't want to hear it.

Sitting in my bed, after having watched four episodes of *Friday Night Lights* in a row, I wondered why I was fighting to stay. I thought of Jean-Paul, the sixty-something man I had had aquatherapy with on a couple of occasions. He would float in the water and only exercise when he thought the physiotherapist was looking. When he found out he was being discharged, he told me, "It's too soon. I should be here at least another two weeks!"

I didn't know what to say. For him, the pain of leaving seemed so much greater than the pain of staying, and yet here I was, acting the exact same way.

Two days after I was told I'd be moved, the executive director of Lyndhurst walked into my room alongside Rumy.

"I'm sorry to have to tell you this, Ruth," she said, "but it's official. You're being transferred to a new unit."

But I'd had time to think and to make other plans.

"I want to be discharged today," I said. "I'm ready to go home."

●

"No. This is crazy. You're not coming home today. Just . . . just no."

I could picture Rich vigorously shaking his head through the phone. I understood his reaction. Up until that very morning, I had felt the same way. Over the past seven months, Rich and I had been incapable of processing anything quickly—not the tingling, the numbness, the deadness in my legs, the drunkenness of my feet, the diagnosis, the surgical outcome, the not-walking, the not-coming-home after surgery, the not-understanding how this tumor had been growing on my back for years and years. We had become used to being pelted with bad news. And now this hard left turn into an open field of freedom was just as shocking. Our brain chemistry had changed. We registered every opportunity, every surprise and change as bad.

"Rich, honey, this time the news is actually good. It's going to be okay."

The last time I said those words was right before I went into surgery, right before I said what I feared was a final good-bye to him. "I'm really ready to come home," I lied. "I am."

"When?"

"I just need to pack up my stuff. That's it."

I looked around my room at the container of Metamucil, three apples, a bottle of cranberry pills, bulk food snacks, writing utensils, my computer, notebook, books. I could literally sweep my arm across my countertop and push everything into an open

205

bag and, along with the few clothes in my closet, I would be good to go.

"What about the rest of your physio?" Rich wanted to know.

"Dr. Zimcik said I could be an outpatient here until my official discharge date."

"Will Amanda be your PT?" He loved her as much as I did.

"Sadly, no. She's just for inpatients. She already dropped by and told me that I'd be working with Mitch. An Aussie guy, apparently very nice."

"I don't like him," Rich said.

I laughed. "I'm sure he's fine."

"How are you going to say good-bye to everyone?"

I had thought about this, too. "I'm not saying any good-byes until I'm finished here for good."

"The kids are going to freak out."

"That's the best part! They're going to come home from school and find me there!"

"They're going to be so happy."

"I hope so."

"Ru?"

"Yeah, babe."

"You're really coming home."

It is either a testament to our kids' resilience, or a comment on the teenage brain's facility to respond to stunning news in the most laid-back fashion possible, but either way, the reunion did not go as I had imagined.

"Oh. Hi," Joey said, when he saw me sitting in the sunroom.

"Well, hi to you, too!" I said.

"Mom!" Henry said, not sure whether this was a crying moment or an I'm-in-trouble moment. "What are you doing here?"

"I got my walking papers, *that's* what I'm doing here!"

"Good job," Joey said.

"Would *anyone* like to hug me?"

They both did and then we let Ellen make snacks for all of us. We ate, we chatted, and then Joey went upstairs, Henry went downstairs, and the reentry process was over. I was back. That was all they needed to know.

For the next five days, I was infused with the same sense of adrenalin and euphoria I had felt after my surgery. No one's life was better than mine. Bit by bit, all my prosaic little joys fell back into place. Dr. Emm had cleared me to drive, so I did that, every day, often for no other reason than that I could. I had to buy a shower chair from a specialty store, but even that didn't bother me; I could still feel autonomy etched into the plastic molding. Henry laughed when I tried to leave his room at bedtime, calling good night over and over since it took me so long just to pull myself up from his bed, straighten out my feet, and maneuver my walker out the door, but I was home and I was happy and there was no need to rush. Ellen stayed on with us to help with the grocery shopping and cleaning and ferrying the kids home from school. But I was there every day when the boys came home, even though their joy at finding me exactly where they had left me that morning may not have been quite as joyful as mine at seeing them. My gratitude for even the tiniest of pleasures was infinite, my spirit indomitable; I'd come through this like a champ. I could do anything. I was an Amazon!

Then Henry forgot his French horn.

Rich had just dropped him off at school on his way to work, but now had to double back home to retrieve the French horn and schlep it to him. In the old days, it would have been me who jumped in the shower and raced down the stairs and ran the French horn up to the school office. But now I stood in the middle of our bedroom on shaky legs, my sensory-impaired feet trying to understand the floor, my butt cheeks flexing to figure out which one needed to activate in order to move my body forward. Rich opened the front door and called upstairs for me, but I was crying too hard to answer. I was free, but free didn't feel at all like I thought it would.

"Ru? Where you at?"

"Upstairs."

"I'm coming up."

I didn't want to be crying. I didn't want to be looking so lame. "I should be the one bringing Henry's stupid French horn back to school!" I yelled.

"It's really not a problem for me to do it, honey."

"I know it's not a problem for you! It's a problem for *me*!"

Rich came over and kissed my face. "You've been home less than a week. Everything will fall back into place."

"When, Rich? When when when when *when*?"

"Soon." He picked up the French horn, kissed me again, and told me he'd see me a little later. I nodded and then went to the bathroom to pull myself together.

Sadness tucked itself in the most banal places. It had been there when I opened a new bar of soap at Lyndhurst; when it was time to change my contact lenses, marking another two weeks' passing; when I ran out of Rich's T-shirts to wear to bed as a substitute for crawling in beside him. Every time I finished the enormous bag of jujubes my mother brought me, there was sadness. When I opened a new tube of toothpaste, there was sadness. Each thing unwrapped, each thing folded and put away, each thing finished and then restarted: sadness. But that was Lyndhurst. Things were supposed to be different now that I was home. And yet, sitting inside the giant black case of my son's forgotten French horn: a giant brass sadness.

·

I decided to go see Dr. Bright, ostensibly to talk about the digestive issues that continued to plague me, but it was more than that. Without my angel nurses around, I was taking questionable measures with my health, like drinking laxative tea every night before bed.

"You need to dial that back," Dr. Bright said.

I came to her office with a notebook full of questions. She sat patiently while I checked them off the list, one by one, until I had only one left.

"I hate to ask this," I said, "but maybe, if it's okay with you, maybe I can book some time in to see you again?"

"I think that's a good idea," she said without hesitation. "Would once a month be okay?"

"I was thinking every two weeks." I was really thinking every two days.

"How about we split the difference and make it every three weeks?"

I looked at the examination table straight ahead of me. I was sitting upright. I didn't need to lie down on it anymore. Everything was sorted out. I was fixed. I was cured. So what if my walk was kind of gimpy and my legs buzzed constantly and my feet felt full of pebbles and my calves felt squeezed by invisible elastic bands? No one could see the complete circuitry breakdown that lay just under my skin. And even if someone did, it wouldn't have mattered—I was standing, I was walking, I was an upright citizen. And yet, I wasn't healed, not really. When would this end? Would I be on nerve medication forever? Would I ever again be the person I once was? Would I ever poo again normally?

"Okay," I said. "Every three weeks." I couldn't look at her. "I'm really sorry. I don't want to be one of 'those' patients."

Dr. Bright put her hand on my leg. I felt proud that my tears stayed in my eyes and that I could go that long without blinking. Dr. Bright reached behind her for the Kleenex box.

"Ruth, your life has completely changed."

"I can't tell my mom when I'm sad anymore." I was barely

speaking above a whisper. "I'm her daughter—she cries when I cry."

"You'll talk to me so you don't have to worry your mom or Rich, okay?"

I nodded: *okay.*

•

Sometimes I forgot I was no longer in a wheelchair. My dreams also hadn't caught up with reality. When I woke up, I had to take a few minutes to figure out where I was and how I got around the house. One morning, while reading the real estate section in *The Globe and Mail*, I became intrigued by a house for sale in Lawrence Park. It was wheelchair accessible with an elevator that went straight from the garage to the second floor. There was a slight ramp leading into the stunning bathroom, and then there was the pearl in the oyster: a marble island low enough to double as a kitchen table so that a wheelchair could be parked there comfortably. I was ready to buy that house right then at the giveaway price of 1.6 million dollars.

Instead, I did a quick and breathless purge of my closet. My shoes had been sitting patiently for months, like forlorn children at an adoption fair waiting quietly for me to pick them. I chose two pairs of sneakers. I gathered up the rest—my beloved high heels, platform boots, summer wedges, even the black flats that I had worn on my anniversary date with Rich—and put them into two recycling bags. I sold them all. My colorful oxford lace-ups had jump-started my new collection, but I needed something more conservative for my cousin's bat mitzvah. I enlisted my sisters to go to the mall with me and help me choose. I tried on flat after flat while they watched me walk across the store.

"Are my feet slipping out of these? Of these? Of these? Of these? Of these?"

I chose a pair of nude and black flats, patent, with a bow. I hated them but my sisters said they did the best job of keeping my feet in lockdown. When we were required to stand during the service, I used the opportunity to do deep-knee bends. My children barely noticed my public exercises anymore.

I continued to think about sex all the time. I was desperate to get the ball rolling again. Rich and I were having sex more, subscribing to the notion of use it or lose it. Although I had to concentrate hard on the mechanics of what we were doing, I was pleasantly surprised to note that in those brief moments when I wasn't wondering *can I feel this, shouldn't I be feeling that?* I was actually starting to register more sensation. The old sensations bore zero resemblance to the new sensations, which now felt like firecrackers flaring up, then fizzling prematurely, leaving me to wonder where all that fiery potential had disappeared to. I stopped thinking of end results; I just rolled with it.

Joel was at the bat mitzvah. I was nervous about seeing him. I must have asked my sisters a dozen times if my left foot was slipping out of my shoe.

"You're fine, Ruthie!" they kept saying.

"Okay," I said, without preamble when I found him. "Wanna watch me?"

He didn't even say "Watch what?" He just nodded. I passed him my mimosa. Then I walked away from him and back toward him. I tried not to favor my right leg. I tried to walk naturally, not with bracing stiffness. I tried to swing my hips, but not with a "catwalk" swing, as the PTs at Lyndhurst referred to it. I tried to walk like someone who didn't have a four-inch scar down her back; like someone who didn't wake up each morning praying for a little poo; like someone who could run up and down the stairs holding a newspaper, a hot cup of coffee, and three clean towels.

"Well?" I said. "Pretty good, right?"

"Very good," he said. He took a sip of his mimosa. "How are your bowel and bladder?"

"Good, good," I said.

"Can you feel anything down there, when you clean yourself?"

"Yes."

"What about everything else . . . down there?"

I blinked several times.

"Sexually," he clarified.

In his hands, the mimosas were as still as a lake at dawn. *He must be an exceptional surgeon*, I thought.

"Well, Joel. Between you and me, it's not what it used to be, but Rich and I are doing it a decent amount just to get something going."

He gave me back my mimosa as though it were a reward for saying the right thing. We walked into the dining hall together.

"But, Joel, this numbness thing in my bum *is* going to go away, isn't it?"

"Yes," he said, in a conversation-ending way. He was on the move, searching for his wife, his mother, his children—anybody who would free him from talking about sex and butt numbness on a Saturday morning in a holy place.

17

The New Normal

New Year's Eve meant I had been home for almost as long as I had been in rehab. I thought that ushering in 2013 meant flushing away the troubles that had riddled me through almost all of 2012. In anticipation of feeling great about what lay ahead, I invited my sister's whole family over to celebrate. At four that afternoon, shortly before they arrived, I called my mother.

"You're not in the mood for having them," she said.

"Why would you even say that?"

"Because I can tell."

"That is not true at all. I'm just concerned that I won't be able to stay up until midnight, at least not in a sitting position. Or a standing position."

"Okay."

"I'm perfectly fine with them coming over."

"Okay."

"God!"

I made garlic bread. I didn't smell it burning because I was mixing the margaritas and the blender was so loud it seemed to block out my sense of smell, but the kids noticed and then I saw smoke and the smoke detector went off and the room filled with fog. I slid over to the oven and took out the burned toast.

"Fuck."

"Mom!" said Henry.

"Sorry, but fuck."

I opened the fridge to get the guacamole and saw Rumy with her latex gloves sitting on the shelf next to the orange juice. I saw myself turn over on the bed. She firmly shoved the magic bullet up my bum. I slammed the fridge shut, but the image remained. I remembered a rumor I heard that Elvis didn't die of a drug addiction but of constipation so intense it brought on a heart attack. My obsession with my bladder and bowel continued, every visit to the bathroom torturous.

By eleven thirty, all the food eaten, the drinks drunk, and the dishes put away, my sister's family went home and our family went upstairs to get ready for bed.

Henry called out. "Where are you, Mom?"

I put on a happy voice. "In the bathroom, honey! Where are you?"

"In your bed!"

I heard him turn on the TV and rustle himself under the covers.

"Oh God oh God oh God," I muttered under my breath. I was sweating.

Eventually, I got up and went to wash my face. I had to sit down to do it. I couldn't stand over the sink with my eyes closed—I lost track of where my body was in space. It was also why I had the shower chair. I couldn't risk closing my eyes while standing up, not even for a second.

I came out of the bathroom. Rich was now in bed with Henry, watching the throngs of people in Times Square waiting for the ball to drop.

"Where's Joey?" I asked.

"Other bathroom."

"Hope he has better luck than me."

"Nice."

A bunch of actors were discussing past New Year's Eves and with whom they had shared kisses. I watched for a couple of minutes. Rich looked at me and smiled and then I went downstairs in the dark. I sat on the top step of the basement stairs. It was fifteen minutes to midnight. I called my mother.

"Mom?"

"What is it, darling?"

I pressed my eyes shut.

"Ruthie?"

I took off my glasses and put them beside me.

"Are you crying?"

I didn't want the kids to hear me.

"Ruthie," my mom said. "You are doing amazing. Just think of how far you've come and how far you're going to go still. I have no doubt whatsoever that you're going to be perfect again—even your bum. I watched you walking down the hall when you were here last week and I was amazed, *amazed* at how well you did. You can't even tell. Honestly. Can you feel me hugging you from here?"

"Yes."

"Actually, I'm surprised you haven't broken down before this."

Rich appeared. He was standing over me, frowning. "It's almost midnight," he said.

I shushed him away, then gave him the thumbs up, then gestured for him to go upstairs to the kids, then shushed him away again. He shook his head, then brought me a Kleenex box. I blew my nose, then gave him the thumbs up twice more.

"Come on!" Joey called from our bedroom. "It's almost midnight!"

"Go. Just go," I said to Rich.

He didn't move, and then he did. I heard him slam the wall before heading upstairs.

"I've heard your mother," my father said, picking up the extension. "And I agree with everything she said. Oh—there goes the ball. Ten, nine, eight . . ."

I was still sobbing.

"Go kiss your wonderful hubby," my mom said.

I said my good-byes and then sat there for a few more minutes before going upstairs. Almost every light was off. Rich and the boys were still awake in our bed. Rich didn't look at me as I came in. I put my hand on his arm and then leaned over him to kiss Henry, then Joey.

"Happy New Year, boys."

And then I kissed Rich, but it was too late.

The kids went to bed and I crawled in beside him and leaned my head on his shoulder. Rich left to go to the bathroom and I followed him. He was standing at the sink and I hugged his back until he turned around and hugged me proper.

"I'm sorry," I said.

"You don't have to apologize."

"I do. I love you."

"I love you, too."

We went to bed and lay there with our eyes open.

"You slammed the wall," I said. "Did you hurt your hand?"

"Since 1995, we haven't missed a kiss on New Year's," he said.

I had rung in the New Year with my parents. I was thinking how hard the year had been for *them* because there is nothing worse than seeing your child in pain. Somewhere in the countdown, I had heard my father say that he wanted to go kiss my mother. I ended up spending the last moment of 2012 alone. I felt sick. My husband, who had done everything for me, while also going to work every day, looking after the kids, updating our family and friends with emails about my progress, keeping on top of what the doctors said, and taking my teary calls at all hours of the day, was denied a kiss at the end of this terrible year because I thought everything was still all about me.

We were back to back. I tried to make it so that our bums touched. They might have been, but I couldn't tell. I pushed my feet toward his. Knowing they rarely hit their target, Rich made sure his feet found mine first. I rubbed them against his, until I had to ask, "Are you wearing socks?"

"Mmmm," he said. He was dozing off.

I started to doze off then, too. I was happy to lie touching him, maybe bum to bum, maybe feet to feet, relieved to know that all was forgiven.

•

"I got the number of this girl you might want to call," Rich told me, shortly after New Year's. "One of my poker friend's friends. Apparently, she had something very similar to what you had."

"That makes me nervous."

"Just take her number. You don't have to call her if you don't want to."

"I *don't* want to."

He gave me her number and I carried it around in my purse for a long time. After my faith-shaking conversation with Carmen back at Lyndhurst, I had decided never again to compare my surgery and progress to others. But my history shows that making a mistake just once isn't enough for me to get the message.

I decided to call this woman, Erin, only after creeping her online first. Her Facebook page showed that she had three children (almost like me!) and was in the arts (just like me!) and loved to climb mountains (not like me!) and go on great family adventures (sort of, almost, just like me!). Still, I proceeded with caution. There remained one red flag that could just as easily have been interpreted as a positive sign: Erin described herself as fully recovered. I was skeptical of this "fully recovered" business. I also presented as "fully recovered." I wasn't. I didn't know if I ever would be. In Erin, I was looking for someone to answer my current, most burning question. I felt confident she could do that.

Erin seemed excited to hear from me, ready to help in whatever way I needed.

"You had a spinal meningioma, right?"

"Yes. Did you?"

"I had an ependymoma."

"What's that?"

"A tumor that developed from cells in the lower back part of my brain."

"How did you know you had that?"

"Excruciating headaches."

"I'm so sorry. That sounds awful."

"I learned some pretty cool stuff about it, though."

I heard some of the words: cells, structures, cavities, canals, something called a lumen. Erin was clearly a card-carrying member of the knowledge-is-power party.

"Do you know I have a website for tumor sufferers?" she asked.

I had looked at it only moments before I called her but immediately regretted it. The stories were heartbreaking; too many issues dovetailed with my own. Even the uplifting posts made me anxious.

"Really? I'll have to take a look at that," I lied. "Listen, did you have numb bum after your surgery?" I blurted.

"Oh God, yes."

"Me, too!" I laughed. "Just tell me when it will go away."

"It will never go away."

"What?"

"It won't."

"But you had your surgery eleven years ago! It must go away eventually."

"But it won't. It never will. And anyway, so what?"

I was miles, months, maybe years, away from "so what."

I thanked her for her time and for sharing her story with me. After, I vowed—again—to never discuss my issues with anyone who appeared to have anything like what I had, and this time I meant it.

I looked at my feet. They were size-7 metaphors, never quite touching the ground, elevating me just slightly to a perfectly functional but wobbly place. I could learn to walk there, to balance there, to sit there, to live there forever if I had to. Time would have to take care of what I couldn't. I needed a new area of focus, something to take my mind off my feet and my numb bum.

My sex life.

There are two mysterious events in my life that I have never been able to solve. The first occurred when I was moving out of the apartment I shared with my friend Fli to move in with my then boyfriend, Rich. While making a quick sweep under my bed to ensure I wasn't leaving anything behind, I discovered a pair of bejeweled slippers with upturned toes. They looked like they belonged to a genie or an Indian princess, or a gay elf.

"Fli!" I called.

She ran up the narrow staircase to my room. "What's the matter?"

I pointed to the twinkling shoes.

"What are those?" she asked.

"You didn't put these under my bed?"

"Huh?"

Later that night, Rich came over and saw the slippers.

"Where did those come from?" Rich asked.

"No idea."

The mystery remained unsolved.

I thought about those slippers when I opened my Kindle one night. I scrolled through all my e-books, which all looked familiar except one, a book called *Taking Instructions*. It came with a warning—something about "Extreme" and "BDSM."

I had a bondage book on my Kindle.

I didn't put it there. I asked Rich. *He* didn't put it there. Joey and Henry—God help me—certainly hadn't put it there, either. It appeared that the same fairy who had placed the jeweled slippers under my bed had returned for some more tomfoolery.

I started reading.

It was raunchy stuff with only the barest bones of a reality-based setup: a studly male teacher, a buxom, naughty female student, and . . . go! I was open to its potential sexual magic almost immediately. Although things *down there* still felt largely frozen, I refused to simply pack it in and live out the rest of my life orgasm-free. I was in possession of eight thousand sensory nerve endings; I would be happy if even half of them worked again.

("I'd be happy with just two," Rich said.)

Like any horny teen, I needed to discuss things with a girlfriend but didn't want to be the one to start the conversation.

Luckily, my friend Beth and I met for breakfast one day. "How's your sex life?" she asked.

"It's good, it's good," I said. "I just can't, you know . . ."

"Really?"

"Really."

"Not even with a vibrator?"

I put my coffee down. "No. But only because I've never used a vibrator."

"You're kidding me."

"Do *you* have one?"

"Do I have *one*?" She sighed. "We're going to the drugstore."

"The *drug*store?"

She knew just what aisle to go to and didn't care who was looking. She grabbed two off the shelf.

"So you can compare and contrast," she explained.

They sat in my bedside table for weeks before I told Rich about them, before I even tried them. I'm not a prude, but somehow, using these (two) vibrators without Rich's knowledge—even though I had been counseled by my friend to take them for a test drive on my own before bringing Rich on board—felt like a betrayal. I needed time to think. Since coming home, I had spent a fair bit of time in our hot tub. The water continued to be a source of soothing and healing. And then one day I remembered to turn the jets on.

A few hundred nerve endings were officially reactivated.

•

Henry and I went for a walk after dinner one night. Since scaling down to one stick from two, I had been advised to switch over and start using the walking stick in my left hand instead of my more dominant right hand to even out my gait. I hated it. Every part of me hated it, especially my left hand and my left leg. My right hand was bereft since its job had been downsized. In an act of pure petulance, it refused to swing when I walked, remaining stiffly by my side, barely budging from my thigh. So I had an idea: I would carry my left stick under my arm like a purse, tapping it on the ground only if I fell into my drunken side-steppy walk. Otherwise, I was pretty much walking without props.

Henry did tricks on his scooter just ahead of me.

"You better be careful, Hen," I warned. "You almost hit yourself with that thing."

"Mom, that's the point! You never know when I'm doing the trick or not!"

I stopped for a couple of minutes to watch him, but even then I didn't lean on my pole. I had been studying how other people walked, taking mental measurements, amazed at how they could put one foot in front of the other so quickly and with such consistency. If there was enough distance between a particularly compelling biped and me, I would try to fall in step with his or her gait, test out his or her walking rhythm against my own to see how it fit. I thought that syncing my steps with the steps of strangers would not only force me to move at a different pace—often one that was faster than my own—but also help me relearn the significance of body language. I was sure that how one walked told the world something interesting about oneself. I was also sure that if Henry didn't stop swinging his scooter around his body like that he was going to slice his ankles off.

"Do me a solid, Hank, and get behind me. Tell me how I look."

I started walking, back ramrod straight. I felt like John Gielgud in every part he ever played.

"You're too stiff," Henry said. "Loosen up a little."

I slackened my knees, rounded out my posture, let my hips do the talking.

"That better?"

"Too much swag."

Swag?

"You mean my hips are moving too much?"

"Way too much."

I split the difference. I felt like I might be approaching something natural.

"There. You look great, Mom."

Not too long after that, I asked Joey to take a walk with me. I told him how excited I was that I had finally regained the art of walking *and* talking while his dad and I were out on our Sunday morning stroll through the neighborhood ravine.

"What I mean is that I didn't have to choose to either do one *or* the other. I could actually *look* at him *while* I was walking. This was a real revelation because, as you know, I haven't been able to do both for the longest time."

"ALL RIGHT ALREADY. I GET IT. THAT'S ALL YOU TALK ABOUT! YOU DON'T HAVE TO ANNOUNCE EVERY SINGLE THING. IT'S ALL YOU TALK ABOUT ALL THE TIME! I GET IT, ALL RIGHT? I GET IT!"

We got home. I opened the door and Joey went straight to the TV. I went straight to the kitchen.

"Did you want some pasta?" I asked him after several minutes of silence.

"Sure."

He came into the kitchen.

"I want a plate," he said. "I mean a bowl. I desire a bowl. I'm desire-a-bowl!"

He sat at the kitchen island and I watched him eat the way he does, with his head bent so far down over the bowl he practically touches it. I didn't see his face again until he was finished.

"You're right," I finally said. "I do talk too much about my recovery."

"It's okay." He wouldn't look at me.

"I guess it's what I think about a lot of the time."

"Of course. I understand that."

"Anyhow, it's really boring and I'm going to try not to do that anymore."

"It's okay, Mom."

"I'm really sorry, Joey."

"Mom, it's okay."

18

Walk It Off

Each morning I took a shower, dried my hair, and put on my makeup; dressed in my workout pants, running bra, workout top, and hoodie; and made my way down to the basement. Walking on the treadmill, although strenuous, never caused a sweat. I meticulously recorded how far and for how long I was able to walk before needing a rest. My limit at Lyndhurst had been twelve minutes, but three months after returning home I was able to complete thirty-two un-pretty minutes. I bobbed and weaved and listed side to side, but I refused to grab hold of the sidebars to steady myself. I bodychecked the wall twice. I looked like a giant drunken boxer throwing punches at an invisible toddler.

I started taking small treks outside without my walking sticks. If I passed my reflection in a store window I stopped to take a look—not at my face but at my feet. Walking toward my reflection in the windows of bus shelters was also an excellent way to keep my feet in check, to ensure I didn't have "swag," that I didn't look too stiff, that my knees were bending just the right amount. And then, the ultimate test: walking past a bunch of construction workers.

I had just left a friend's place when I saw a convoy of trucks parked on the street, thick hoses stretched out beneath them. Men in sunglasses and orange reflector vests hung around with their legs spread wide. There was very little sidewalk for me to navigate, so I asked one of the men if it would be okay if I walked around the trucks and into the road so I could get to my car. I was graciously waved ahead. I tried to play it cool, to walk smoothly, to not veer too dramatically to one side or the other, when I heard it: an unmistakable *woo-hoo* kind of whistle, one that lingered on both the woo *and* the *hoo*. This was a solid "I'm just appreciating the view" whistle. Maybe, probably, definitely, there was a far younger, far more attractive woman walking right behind me who was the real object of their whistles, but I couldn't risk turning around to look. And anyway, just the thought that I was whistle-worthy motivated me to keep taking these treks outside, alone, without my sticks.

This taste of independence was the sweetest I'd ever known. Soon after that walk, I took a road trip by myself to visit my friend Paula, who had left for Alberta to start a new life just before I left for St. Mike's to start mine, which meant she was one of the blessed few who had never seen me in a wheelchair. Our reunion took place in Guelph where she was visiting her mother. She ran out to meet me in the driveway. We hugged like long-lost lovers. I had forgotten to warn her that hugging was easy but letting go could throw me off balance. Luckily, Paula was the kind of hugger who let go with every part of her body except her hands, which she used to grasp my arms and hold me in place to take a good, long look at me. She didn't let go of me all the way up the stairs and into the house.

"Paula," I said. She was gripping me so hard it was starting to hurt. "I *can* walk by myself, you know."

"Shut up. I'm not doing this for you. This is for me."

Once inside, I walked around for her.

"I don't see any difference," she said, slapping her thighs. "No difference at all."

Paula and I had worked together on a television series for several years. She is an excellent actress, which meant I couldn't tell if she was lying.

"Really? You can't see *any* difference in my walking between then and now?"

"None."

We drank an entire bottle of wine and then fell asleep around midnight, mid-sentence. For the first time in a long time, I was pleasantly—not maddeningly—buzzed.

At home, having a glass of wine with dinner was fine. When my coordination felt wonky, I just parked myself on the nearest couch. But drinking away from home was another matter entirely. I was concerned that my new feet might become that secretary at the office Christmas party who, after one too many mojitos, ends up in the broom closet making out with her boss's wife.

Then, one day, Rich announced that the two-time flower-sending movie star and his famous director wife had invited us out to dinner.

"That might be fun!" I meant it. I was excited to dress up and show off how well I was walking.

But after only one martini, I knew I was in trouble.

"When I drink, I don't walk very well," I confided to the movie star, who was sitting next to me, but I couldn't tell if he had heard me or not.

The meal ended. I bent down to get my purse. I put my scarf around my neck and gingerly pulled my jacket on. My back was sparking, a warning that the steel rods would soon be forcing their way up between my shoulder blades. I pushed my chair far back so I would have plenty of room to stand. I unbent my legs slowly.

The tension in my back and chest was unbearable. *What will my first step away from the table look like? And where the hell are my feet?* I surreptitiously checked under the table to make sure they hadn't migrated up the famous director's pant leg. I wasn't drunk, but my feet might make me look like I was.

We partnered off for the walk to our cars. I was with the movie star. The whole way, I walked like a crazy person. I farted frequently. I was fairly certain the latter was lost on him (if not on Rich and the famous director walking right behind us), but my loopy walking couldn't have possibly gone unnoticed. My ankles kept slamming into each other like I was walking in a canoe. I banged into the movie star. If I had been with anyone else, I would have blamed my inebriated feet, laughed about it, slipped my arm through theirs, and moved on. I don't know if the movie star's absence of a helpful arm was because he really didn't notice anything out of the ordinary or because he noticed but, kindly, didn't want to embarrass me. Either way, I was furious.

On the ride home, I ranted to Rich about this perceived insensitivity to my needs.

"Honestly," Rich said. "Why do you hate him so much?"

"I don't hate him." In fact, I thought he was wonderful. But there was no denying that he stirred me up. I didn't want to say it out loud, but the truth was that he underscored that my career was in limbo.

Lying in bed that night, with my drunken feet passed out below me, I wondered if I would ever act again, and if I didn't, what on earth was I going to do?

•

"I have an announcement and a question," I said to Dr. Bright during one of our frequent appointments.

"I'm ready."

"Rich booked us a trip to Las Vegas!"

"Fantastic! You've been before, right?"

"Many times. We love it. So that should be good. It's three months away. End of May. I think I should be perfect by then, don't you?"

She laughed but didn't answer. "What's the question?"

"It's about my wheelchair permit."

I don't remember the day that I officially began walking on my own without the aid of a stick, only that it snuck up on me so gradually it was several days before I realized I didn't even know where my sticks were. But I still had my wheelchair permit. Six months had passed since it had been issued, which meant it was either time to renew it or give it up. What had originally felt so shameful, so demoralizing, so necessary, now just felt like a crutch.

"It's up to you," Dr. Bright said. "If you want me to sign the renewal papers, I'm happy to."

The winter had been hard. I was constantly on the lookout for black ice. I was terrified of falling. "Maybe just for another six months?"

I left the appointment with the papers signed and drove to Service Ontario. I parked my car and walked the remaining block to the license office. It happened to be just a couple of doors away from the Starbucks closest to Lyndhurst where I had routinely gone with Joey and other visitors. I felt triumphant, strolling back through my temporary old 'hood wearing a long black pair of boots with the tiniest of stacked heels. I had only just started wearing them. They were lined with fake fur, precluding the need for dreaded socks. The boots made me feel like my old self.

The sidewalks were clear and dry even though there had been a massive snowstorm days earlier. I was thinking about where I might go for lunch and who I might corral to join me, when I crashed. I don't remember the fall, only the hard bounce of my mouth on the sidewalk and the sharp smack of my sunglasses cutting through the bridge of my nose. I couldn't get up. One arm of my glasses was around my ear, the other pushed up to the top of my head. I was sure my teeth had gone clean through my lip. My face was burning. I blinked several times. I could see three pairs of shoes very close to my cheek.

"Are you okay?"

"Oh my God!"

"Can I help you?"

"I, I can't. Just gimme a second. I need . . . uh, I don't really walk very well."

Somebody lifted me up and helped me into the paint store I had tripped in front of. My helper gently sat me down at the table at the front of the store and offered me some water. I accepted and then I took off my glasses, covered my eyes with my hands and burst into tears. The man tried to soothe me.

"I'm so embarrassed. So humiliated."

"No, no, ma'am," he said. "No."

And then the whole story—*all* of it—tumbled out of me. I told this poor stranger about the tumor, the surgery, Lyndhurst, recovery, walking, wheelchair permit. I don't know why I kept going; I don't know why or when I stopped.

"Is something going on with my face?" I finally asked. "Am I bleeding?"

I looked up so he could assess me. *Shawn* was written in cursive on a badge sewn to his shirt.

"Well," Shawn said. "You're bleeding a little."

"Where?"

He pointed to my forehead and the bridge of my nose.

"Do you have a mirror, please? A washroom, please?"

"Of course, ma'am."

He walked me there. I passed two employees with their names

also embroidered on their shirts. They looked at me, then quickly looked away. Were they the ones who had helped me off the sidewalk? Instead of asking, I just tried to bleed a little less as I walked past. I looked in the bathroom mirror and a sad-sad face stared back at me. I was full of cuts and blood. What kind of woman falls flat on her face on the bone-dry sidewalk and then can't get up on her own? What kind of woman babbles and blubbers and bleeds in front of strangers? What kind of woman tells a perfect stranger her long-winded tale of woe without even being asked? Only one kind: a divorcée who eats Xanax for breakfast and gets plastered while her children are in school. I dabbed at my bloody nose and forehead. I pressed some wet paper towel to my burning lips, and then I walked the gauntlet back to Shawn.

"Thank you, Shawn," I said. "You're so kind. I'm sorry about all this."

"No, no, ma'am. Not at all, ma'am."

I left the store on shaky feet.

Service Ontario was right next door. If I was worried about them questioning the renewal of my permit based on how well I was walking, I'd pretty much taken care of that problem. My jeans were ripped right through on both knees. I didn't even care. I kept my sunglasses on. The right lens was all scratched up. It was uncomfortable to stand. I had "sway," as Mitch, my outpatient physiotherapist at Lyndhurst, called it, which meant that my ankles couldn't keep still, always ready to do a little dance, shake a leg, drop to the ground.

The line moved forward and I moved with it. I don't know if anyone was looking at me. At Lyndhurst, I had perfected the art of looking straight ahead. Once at the front of the line, I pushed my permit renewal toward the woman behind the counter.

"We'll send the new permit in the mail," she said.

"Okay."

I waited for her to say something else, to ask me if I was okay so I could barf out my entire story to her, too, but she had already gestured toward the next person in line.

As I walked back to my car, I searched for the huge obstacle that had obviously tripped me. There was none, only flat pavement. My body had betrayed me.

I called Rich from the car, sobbing.

"I broke my face and now no one will look at me! I carry myself like I'm luggage too difficult to lift. And listen to me, listen to what I've become! My response to *everything* is to cry first, process later. And the kids are going to come home from school and take one look at my face and think, 'That lady's damaged goods.' And I'm scared, Rich. I'm scared you're going to die. I miss my old life. I want to live long enough to grow old." I stopped at a red light and looked at the driver in the car next to me. He was looking straight ahead and singing with gusto to the radio. "I feel so old, Rich."

He listened to me for the entire drive home.

"Go inside and rest," he said.

"Okay."

I went straight upstairs, took a bath, then got into bed and pulled the covers over my head. I closed my eyes and wished I was more religious. I wished I could conjure a psalm or a biblical verse to console myself. The only one I knew by heart was the middle section of the twenty-third psalm—*Even though I walk through the valley of the shadow of death, I will fear no evil, for you are with me; your rod and your staff, they comfort me.* It helped. It also made me think of a stranger I had met at the bookstore just a few days earlier. He looked like what I imagined God to look like. He had a fuzzy gray beard and matching fuzzy gray hair and round wire-rimmed glasses. His teeth leaned this way and that, but still, he had a whiff of the regal about him.

"That is a really beautiful cane you're holding," I told him.

It was my first week leaving the house without my stick. I felt vulnerable without it.

"Since I've had this old piece of driftwood," he said, tapping it lovingly, like it was his pet, "I get stopped by about two women a day. Do you know where Picton is?"

"I think so," I said.

"I have a place out there. If you walk along the shoreline you'll find lots of these."

"May I touch it?"

I was wearing my heavy winter boots that laced halfway up my calves and sported some serious treads. They held my feet in pretty well but they weighed a ton and standing too long in one spot made me wobble like a Weeble. I touched his cane. It was beautifully shaped and sanded down. It even had a handle and a nice flat bottom.

"Thank you," I said.

He smiled a wide, knowing smile and winked at me.

Thinking about that Godly man, I felt calmer. The kids would be home from school soon. I needed to get out of bed, wash my face, and pull myself together. When they saw me, I knew exactly what I would say: "Who wants pizza for dinner?"

19

Something Old, Something New

One morning, I woke up and turned on my computer. My picture was finally back up on my IMDb page—just the sign I'd been waiting for. I called my agent.

"I'm back!" I told her.

Within days, I got a TV audition. I settled into my chair by the fireplace and highlighted my lines. The role was a nurse trying to subdue a patient; patient grabs nurse, nurse fights back, someone runs for help and the scene is over. Only two pages, probably only one day's work, totally doable.

"Just one minor thing," I told my agent. "A stupid thing. It probably won't even matter, but does this patient really grab me? If so, I'll go down like a house of cards. I'm not kidding. I won't be able to stay up straight."

"Hmmm. Let me call the casting director."

Twenty minutes later, she called back.

"I think we'll take a pass on this audition."

"I'm really sorry," I said.

"No problem at all. We'll get you next time."

"Sure."

Next time came fairly quickly. The audition was for the part of a lawyer and called for her to chase down a client in a corridor.

I called my agent.

"Err, Jennifer? I'm not quite at the running-down-a-hall stage yet."

"No problem. We'll take a pass on this one, too. Something else will come up."

"Sure, sure."

I started to dread the phone ringing. Every audition, no matter how innocuous it seemed on a first reading, was laced with traps. But then *Degrassi*, my long-time employer, came calling. The storyline was a variation on a theme: Daughter in trouble, Daughter needs Mother (me). But this time the story hit alarmingly close to home: Daughter finds a lump on her back. Mom delivers the news that it's cancer, Mom tells Daughter she'll be with her every day in hospital, Daughter has another MRI, Mom delivers the amazing results that the cancer is gone.

I am a terrible TV crier. Something inside me seizes up, refusing to unleash the tears. It would have been hard for any of my former nurses to believe this considering I cried at the opening of a Kleenex box. But this time, in this scene, the floodgates gave way. Tears pinged my eyes. I didn't even have to yawn first—the only old trick in my bag. All I had to do was think about my own MRI results and how devastating the news had been for my parents and tears rolled down my face.

I nailed the scene. It was a thrill. But the thrill of that moment was quickly replaced by an unassailable set of concerns. I needed to rest my legs but was too shy to ask for a chair. I needed my gabapentin, but there was no time for me to take it before blocking the next scene. My shoes kept slipping off my feet when I wasn't looking. My back was starting to ping and pop, a warning that things were only going to get worse. The buzzing in my legs was reaching a fever pitch. And worst of all/best of all, no one noticed my distress.

We had one shot left in the day. It was a close-up of my daughter, which meant that I was needed for her eyeline but wouldn't be seen in the frame. An apple box was set up right behind the camera for me to sit on. I was so relieved not to have to stand . . . until I saw the seat of the apple box. It was tiny—not too tiny for a regular-size bum, which is more or less what I have—but my bum now felt three times bigger. How was I going to sit on that box without rolling off it? I stared at it long enough for the first assistant director to clue in.

"Hold on!" he yelled, before running off to get me a pillow.

He put it on the apple box. "Will that be more comfortable for you, Ruth?"

I started sweating. Using a pillow would only make things worse—it was too puffy. My bum would register its texture as bubble wrap. All eyes were on me; everyone wanted to get the shot over with so we could all go home.

"That's perfect! Thank you so much."

The first AD held his hand out so I could step over the cables and lower myself down onto the box. My stress level was so high throughout my TV daughter's close-up, it was a breeze to cry again, take after take, just to release some tension, even though *the camera wasn't even on me*. When they called "That's a wrap!" I put my head in my hands and blew out all my held-in breath.

I came home and sat quietly in my chair by the fireplace, still in full-on TV makeup, still coiffed with my TV hair. I thought about the last few months and about how much had changed, and I asked myself the same question that Dr. Zimcik had been required to ask me every few days: *What are your goals?* Although I couldn't say for sure what my next goal was, I now knew what it wasn't.

I picked up the phone and called my agent. "Jennifer?" I said. "I'm all done."

•

I needed to see a doctor before I went to Las Vegas, but Dr. Bright was on vacation. Nothing was terribly wrong, but I'd been a month without seeing a professional and that left me alone for too long with my imagination and the Internet to aid in my unraveling.

"You can see Dr. Calum," I was told by the receptionist.

"What's Dr. Calum's first name?" I asked, fishing for the good doctor's gender.

"John."

Ah. So I would be discussing my bowel movements with a man. Fine. I sat in the waiting room and pulled out my food journal so I could refer to it in our appointment. For months, I had been keeping diligent track of what went in and out of my body—both food-wise and medication-wise.

Dr. Calum was tall and polished. He wore glasses and a light pink button-down shirt with an official white lab coat. We sat down in Dr. Bright's office.

I heaved a big sigh and asked, "Are you prepared to talk about poop for a while?"

"I'm fine with that." He opened up a grainy brown folder.

I gave him the Cliffs Notes version of my surgery. I spoke respectfully of my tumor, using its proper name—meningioma. My friend Sheryl preferred it when I called it that. She said it sounded like a nice pasta.

I finished my story. Dr. Calum's face was serious. He jotted some notes in his file.

"I'm here today largely because of the bloating," I said. "I can't take it anymore. I look—I *feel*—three months pregnant."

"I want to say something, but my mind is drawing a complete blank," he said.

I waited while he rolled his chair over to the computer. He typed in some words and then said *okay* and rolled his chair back.

"I'm guessing you want to do things naturally, is that right?"

"Absolutely," I said. "I've had enough with the drugs already."

He suggested peppermint oil that he could only find on UK websites. "Colpermin. That's the name I was trying to remember— the name of that peppermint oil."

"I thought doctors weren't allowed to have lapses like that," I said, thinking he was one of those jokey-type of doctors, but he wasn't. What he was, was a good listener.

We talked for a while about the pluses of adding peppermint oil to my regimen. I told him how I ate three pieces of natural black licorice every night. I asked him if this could be problematic for my digestive system. He assured me that there was no documented medical fallout from eating black licorice. I told him about Rich's and my upcoming trip to Las Vegas and how I was nervous about disrupting my eating routine and if he had any suggestions for me and if I should take a laxative while I was there and what did he think about the continued use of stool softeners and if he thought I was eating enough fiber or maybe I was eating too much fiber and did he think I could develop a dependency on all that over-the-counter poop stuff and should I take my homemade granola with me and would my belly ever go down and was it normal to feel so happy when I tooted even when it was entirely inappropriate and would I ever feel normalish again?

"May I say something?" he asked.

I said nothing.

"You've obviously been through a lot. Let me ask you this: Have things gotten better?"

"You mean down there?" I pointed to my bum.

"Yes," he said.

I mentally zipped through my progress and then to my surprise, I said, "Yes." Things had improved, were *continuing* to improve.

"Okay. I think you should put your food journal away and enjoy yourself. Going to Las Vegas is supposed to be fun. You need to put your worries aside."

I shook my head and stared into my lap.

"You don't even know," I said. "I've gone from worrying about why my feet tingle to wondering if I'll die on the operating table to wondering if I'll ever walk again to worrying about my kids to wondering if I'll ever be able to figure out where the edges of a fucking *chair* are again with my stupid tingling bum—" I stopped for a second to get my train of thought back. "This current worry of mine is like a *gift* compared to everything else that came before it."

And then the tears came rolling down the river of my cheeks. It wasn't Dr. Calum or Dr. Zimcik or Dr. Bright or even the doctor's office that unleashed them. It was living. As long as I was living, I was going to cry.

"I hear you, Ruth. I hear you," Dr. Calum said. And I believe he really did.

I barely picked up my food journal after that.

•

My greatest concern when anticipating our trip to Las Vegas was also my silliest: that I wouldn't be able to hoist myself up onto the stools around the card tables. But thinking about the stools distracted me from my even bigger concern, which was the endless walking I would have to do to get from our room to the casino to the pool to the restaurant. Even in my assortment of sensible footwear, I couldn't guarantee that I wouldn't either tire or trip or roll over on my ankles. I worried about maintaining my strict routine of drinking lemon water before bed and first thing in the morning, careful to leave exactly half an hour before drinking my first cup of coffee in the hopes of kick-starting my digestive system. Even with Dr. Calum's sage words in my head, I worried about not having exactly the right granola with exactly the right yogurt for breakfast. I hated in advance the terrible choice I might have to make between having a second martini and being able to walk away from a table without veering sharply into another drunk guest.

I also worried that my worrying might ruin our trip.

In the end, my worries disappeared upon arrival. It was thrilling to be with Rich in a big, fancy hotel for the first time since all the *tsurris* had begun. But then I remembered Rich *had* been to a hotel without me, under less joyful circumstances.

While I was in surgery, he had slipped out of the waiting room and walked over to The King Eddy. That was the moment my story spun away from me and sliced sharply into his. I could only guess what his ordeal—as a result of mine—must have been like. I wondered: Did people remember to ask him how *he* was doing? Did *I*?

I pictured Rich trying to remember which room we had had our wedding reception in and then, with a jolt of memory, climbing the staircase with the gleaming gold banister. Or maybe it wasn't gleaming anymore. Maybe he was thinking the same thing about us— that our once glossy life had lost its patina, giving way to a lesser shine, one that gleamed faintly under a series of fresh dings and scratches. Many times, over the last several months, I had wanted to ask Rich what he was thinking when he went back there. Was it: *What if her toes don't move? What if she never walks again? What if our relationship is never the same?* How could he not have wondered, while looking around the same ballroom where we had been tossed in the air clinging to our chairs: *Did the tumor start growing here before our lives together had even begun?*

Up until a few months earlier, it was unimaginable that we

would ever be in Vegas at a gorgeous hotel again, the weekend stretching out luxuriously in front of us. In typical Vegas fashion, the dream actually matched the reality.

Near the end of our weekend, I sat at a three-card poker table next to Jersey Girl. She had outstanding arms and I told her so.

"Do you work out a lot?" I asked. Her arms were not just muscular, but smooth and long and brown.

"I used to work out all the time, every day, actually, but I don't really anymore."

"How come?"

Rich joined us at the table. The weekend might have been winding down but we certainly weren't.

"I'm disabled."

Rich and I turned to her. I could feel us both thinking the same word: *Where?*

"I have braces on my legs."

I pulled back from my stool and looked under the table, about as subtle as Las Vegas itself. There were her legs, two plastic braces from her knees to her ankles, holding them upright.

"The worst part is I can't wear heels anymore," she said.

"Neither can I!" I said.

"Tell her," Rich prodded me. "Tell her!"

I summed up my saga in record time; I was far more interested in hearing hers. But as I spoke, she nodded her head as if this was familiar to her. She had discovered after the birth of her second son (she also had two boys, the exact ages of ours) that she had drop foot. She was on the treadmill at her gym when a fellow runner on the treadmill behind her pointed it out. Like me, she knew something was wrong but was too scared to address it right away. It turned out she had a diagnosis with such a long name she didn't even bother telling me, using the five-letter acronym instead. It wasn't terminal bad, just terrible-bad-luck bad.

We swapped stories about gabapentin and our respective dosages.

"Oh!" she said suddenly and then started digging around in her purse. "I forgot I have to take my drugs now. The time difference has me all screwed up."

"Me, too!" I said. I had set my phone alarm for three times a day as a reminder.

We talked about the angst surrounding footwear and our sons' future bar mitzvahs. We talked about camp and how most of the non-Jews we knew just couldn't understand why we shipped our kids away for the entire summer. We talked Jew to Jew, woman to woman, disabled person to disabled person, and then it was time for Rich and me to go.

I was wearing a short black dress and flat gladiator sandals, legs on full display. I slid off the stool and took a moment to ease the stiffness out of my legs before taking that first step, always the trickiest one. Rich put his arm around me and I put my arm around him. As we walked away, I could feel Jersey Girl's eyes pinned to my calves, which were back to being as strong and curvy as they once were—more cows than calves, really—and I felt self-conscious in a new way. I didn't want to walk well—it felt show-offy, rude.

"Chinese for dinner?" I asked, once we were outside the casino.

"It's Sunday night," said Rich. "Of course Chinese."

I resisted the urge to race back to Jersey Girl, to hug her, to tell her how beautiful she was, to insist, without really knowing anything at all, that everything was going to be okay.

EPILOGUE

A Rich Life

Everything was going to be okay.

Almost a full year had passed since I had gone into the hospital, which meant it was time for an MRI, which would tell me if I was tumor-free, or not. I went into the capsule, came out of the capsule, and then, hours later, it was time to get the results.

Meningiomas can be rascals. At the end of every egg-shaped tumor is a little dural tail, a tail that can complicate a surgery, a tail that a surgeon sometimes has to leave behind in order to keep as much of the nervous system intact as possible. If left to their own devices, however, these tails can grow into new meningiomas. Dr. Ginsberg was fairly confident he had been able to remove my entire tumor, including the tail, but he couldn't be sure without an MRI.

I tried not to be afraid of the results. Not after what had recently happened.

I had returned to Lyndhurst for my final outpatient appointment with PT Mitch, wearing a new pair of bright blue Nikes. My feet continued to feel crazy but they sure looked happy. I signed in for my appointment with the sour-looking receptionist in the outpatient clinic who, as it turned out, was not sour at all. (At Lyndhurst, nothing was ever as it first appeared, except for the latex gloves.)

"You look so nice!" I told the receptionist, commenting on her sleeveless, belted sweater dress. "Going on a date after work?"

She snorted. "Does having dinner with my dad count?"

I smiled. *Not really*, I thought.

"All signed in, Ruth," she said for the last time.

PT Mitch was already waiting for me in the small outpatient gym.

"Too bad the weather's not better," he said.

"Why? Were you hoping to go for a run?" I asked.

"I was, yeh." He was sounding particularly Australian that day.

I leaned back so I could see out the window. A little gray. A little drizzly. A little windy.

"Looks perfectly fine to me," I said with a shrug.

"Yeh?"

"Yeh. Let's do it, Mitch! Let's go for that run!"

We walked past the wheelies, past the cafeteria, past the leather settee by the elevators and through the automatic doors that led to the smoker's gazebo. I passed the picnic table where I used to read my paper and eat my apples. I thought about how on weekends, while I waited for visitors, I'd position my wheelchair at the end of that table, then lock my wheels into place. I'd take my wipes and paper towel out of my purse and set them on the table with my apple on top to keep them from blowing away, then I'd take off my shoes and socks and set them neatly beside my right wheel. I'd eyeball the distance from me to the table and then make some adjustments with my wheels. I would pull my bum a little closer to the edge of the seat until, trying my best not to use the arms of the chair for support, I would stand up and *dig* my feet into the cold, damp dirt. I didn't care how cold my feet got, or how dirty—that's what the wipes were for. The point always was to feel feel *feel*, so I would dig dig *dig*. After, I would sit down to give my jelly legs a break, but only for a moment. I would repeat this exercise over and over again until grounding myself started to mean more than just grinding my feet.

In those early days, I'd often see Rei out there, working harder than anyone I'd ever known, every single day, no matter what mood he might have been in—and he must have been in a bad mood sometimes. He never stopped moving, no matter how feeble his right foot looked. He was my inspiration. He never failed to tell me how well I was doing, even when I knew otherwise.

I didn't tell Mitch any of this. He was wearing his hoodie and worn-in chinos and hipster sneakers. His hands were thrust inside his pockets. It was cold, a little blustery, the wind delivering the occasional *shpritz* of spring rain.

"You ready?"

"Let's do it!"

My gusto was not matched by my speed, which was so slow that Mitch finally gave up all pretense of running alongside me and down-geared to a pleasant walk. My arms were pumping and my legs were hopping up and down like a Monty Python imitation of someone running. I didn't care. I ran down the slight incline toward the ravine where I used to watch all the dogs and their owners. There were days at Lyndhurst when I would get a burst of energy and roll down the path in my wheelchair, the path that Mitch and I were now running on. Getting down was always easy. I'd let go of the wheels and glide. Wind would blow through my hair. My chair would stop on its own close to the gates that opened up onto the ravine. At this point I would have only one choice: to get back up that hill. The problem was, I had very little arm strength to do so. On more than one occasion I had to swallow my rising panic. I dreaded the thought of one of the dog walkers or moms asking if I needed help. It was bad enough needing my own children to push me around; someone else's child would have undone me for sure. Somehow, despite my skinny arms and blistered hands, I would make it up the incline to the picnic table where I had started, feeling both triumphant and deflated: all that effort and still in a wheelchair.

But a kind of magic was happening now with Mitch. Every time he asked, "Would you like to turn here?" I'd say, "Sure, Mitch! Why not?" I hopped over puddles, jumped up onto the curb, circumnavigated potholes and gravel. We ran out through the Lyndhurst gates and onto a full-fledged street. We dodged garbage cans and debris.

"You're going faster now," Mitch said and he started to run with me. And then, "Let's turn back here."

Maybe he'd had enough. Ha! I hadn't. I picked up speed as I ran back through the Lyndhurst gates. In on a gurney, out on my feet.

We walked together through the lobby and back to the outpatient area. Amanda, my original PT, came out of her office at just that moment to meet us. She was beaming.

"So," I said, a little breathlessly, "I guess that's it, then."

"I guess so, Ruth," said Mitch, who was smiling proudly.

I put my hands on my hips and looked down at the ground.

"Thank you both so much, for everything you did for me." I was crying when I looked at Amanda. Turns out that punky girl I had met was wrong: It wasn't Neil who was the best PT for me, it was Amanda.

I gathered up my coat and my knapsack. I blew them both a kiss good-bye and then, for the last time, I left Lyndhurst.

•

As we sat in the neurology department of St. Mike's awaiting the results of my MRI, an older gentleman came into the room with his wife. He was using his walker and moving at a decent pace. He took a seat and his wife folded herself down beside him and took up her newspaper. She had a light smile on her face, prepared for all outcomes.

In the seat across from us was a youngish man wearing a baseball cap. He was sitting forward holding his cane, and every so often he'd wince and then switch positions.

"He doesn't know where his bum is," I whispered to Rich. "I can tell."

Rich glanced over, but he seemed lost in thought.

His hands were empty. "Didn't you bring something to read? Why don't you go downstairs and grab a newspaper, babe?"

"I don't need anything," he said. "I don't want to miss you being called in."

I put my hand on his leg.

I opened my purse and foraged for a Werthers. I didn't feel like writing or reading, either. I wasn't scared. But in case Rich thought I was, I wanted to—in a relaxed fashion—suck on my candy and mull over the year. I thought about a walk I had recently taken with my friend Fli and her highly anxious dog, Nunu. The three of us moved in a tight little pack.

"People keep telling me how I must have been transformed by this experience," I said.

"Have you been?"

"I guess so. I move differently—obviously—so physically, yes, I feel completely other—but ultimately, I'm the same old cow I was before."

"Listen to me. Transforming means you've *gone through* something. It doesn't mean you got stuck someplace in the middle, for Christ's sake!" she said. The year had transformed Fli, I saw. She had grown protective and righteous on my behalf. "You went through this thing, you dusted yourself off, and here you are. Still you."

It would have been nice to think that a life-changing event actually did change my life in some profound way, but it was a greater relief to see how much of my life remained the same. I was just happy to have lived to tell the tale, happy to report: *I'm not dead, all good.*

But the truth was somewhat more complicated. There was no denying a transformation of sorts *had* taken place. I had slowed down. I learned that not only was it okay to do just one thing at a time, instead of scrambling to accomplish myriad tasks at once, but that it made me feel calmer. Being slower was actually a gift, much like the wheelchair permit for my car. I didn't take walking for granted anymore, either, but I looked forward to the day when I might again. I still had to work hard to keep my left leg from swinging out when I walked—the shuffle that Joel had alluded to while I was still at Lyndhurst—but my mirror told me that improvements were being made daily. And as far as I could tell, the kids had emerged from my absence not only unscathed, but happy. Rich and I had only grown closer.

I looked at him. He was leaning his right elbow on his thigh, two fingers pressed up against his lips, thinking about I could only imagine what.

"Rich," I said. "Do you remember when Joey called me from his pal Ethan's house while I was in the hospital and Ethan yelled out: 'Tell your mom I send her my condolences,' and I yelled back, 'Thank you, Ethan, but I'm not dead?' "

Rich nodded his head and let loose a tiny laugh.

"Or when you worried that my roommate at St. Mike's would yell 'get a room' if you got into bed with me?"

"Correction. I thought she would yell: 'get a *private* room.' "

We laughed a little more.

"Did you give the nurses all the cards you wrote?" he asked me.

"I did. I was sad Rumy wasn't around, though, to say good-bye."

"You loved her."

"I loved all of them."

He leaned over to kiss me, but his phone rang in his pocket and he jumped and took the call down the hall. As soon as he left, Dr. Ginsberg called me in.

We had barely taken our seats when I said, "Guess what I did this morning?"

"What?"

"I went for a half-hour run."

"That's great!" he said with generalized enthusiasm.

I waited.

"Hold on. What?"

"I went for a run."

He looked up at me with fresher, clearer eyes.

"That's remarkable," he said.

"Thank you."

Rich ran into the room, breathless. Dr. Ginsberg and I continued to chat.

"Sorry to *interrupt*," Rich said. "But have you told Ruth the results of her MRI yet?"

Dr. Ginsberg looked at his file. "No," he said. "Not yet."

I sat very still—stillness being a proven shield against bad news.

"It's all clean," he said.

Rich brushed his hands over his eyes, then reached for my arm.

"I knew it," I said. "I knew it would be good. Told you I wasn't scared."

I was petrified.

Technical medical talk ensued. The MRI showed that the dura, the protective coating around my spine, was thickened but that was likely scar tissue and was not an indicator of anything sinister. There was no compression of the spinal cord, and, most significantly, the dural tail had been fully excised, which meant no residual meningioma. Rich had questions about the possibility of my getting a new tumor, but he didn't use the word *tumor*. He stuck to the more precise "meningioma," saying it over and over again. He leaned forward, his intense hazel eyes fixed on Dr. Ginsberg, pinning him. The office throbbed with Rich's worry. One would think he couldn't live without me when in fact the exact opposite was true. There was nothing Rich couldn't do. Finally, it was my turn to ask Dr. Ginsberg all my unanswerable questions.

When will my bum get better?

When will everything about my bum work better?

When can I stop taking the gabapentin?

When will my left leg stop feeling thick and staticky?

When can I get my old feet back?

When when when?

He didn't have any answers; I didn't expect him to. His job as a surgeon was done. But I would ask him again next year, and the year after that, and the year after that. I would need follow-up MRIs for the next ten years.

Rich and I walked back to the car. I was having a bad bum day and my legs felt like the inside of a garment factory during the busiest shift. I squirmed in my seat. As we drove away, I found my thoughts traveling back to—of all people—the neurologist, Dr. Shure.

She had called the house twice while I was still at Lyndhurst, left messages with Joey, asked that I *please* call her back. I didn't. I knew she felt badly about missing the signs of my tumor. I knew she wanted to know how I was doing. I knew that, while she had tried her best, she had also been sidetracked by my skinny arms and big calves. But who knows? Had she been quicker off the mark I might have had the surgery sooner with another surgeon— one less patient, less brilliant than Dr. Ginsberg, one who didn't have my worried cousin breathing down his neck. Maybe, if my tumor had been discovered sooner, I would have been living my life from a wheelchair permanently. In retrospect, maybe I should have returned her call: to thank her.

I thought about my beloved Dr. Zimcik and how hard it had been to say good-bye to her, even though I couldn't wait to go home, how she had hugged me hard and given me her email address and told me to stay in touch. She must have known I loved her.

I thought about all my fellow patients whom I had planned on saying good-bye to: Arpita, Rei, Derek, even The Captain. But like so many patients before me, I'm sure, I left without looking back.

I thought about the hundreds of pages I had filled while I was at the hospital and later at Lyndhurst, about how I would some-times look at my fellow patients and wonder: *Are you writing it all down, too?* I thought, since I'm not acting anymore, maybe I could do something with those pages.

"I have to call my folks," I said to Rich. "Right now."

Since I had been at Lyndhurst, a new routine had developed: I was not allowed to say a word until both my mom and dad were on the line. Every conversation now happened in stereo. "Mom?"

"Hold on, Ruthie. Larry, pick up the phone!"

"I'm here, I'm here!" my dad said from the extension.

I had to hold the phone away from my ear. "I'll keep it short," I said, knowing they were waiting. "It's all clear. No more tumor."

"That's wonderful/oh thank God/what did Dr. Ginsberg/are you on your/is Rich with/you're yelling in my ear, Fran!/you're yelling in my ear!"

After I hung up, I thought about how hard it was to be a parent, how it would never be easy—for any of us.

But still, the future looked promising.

I didn't know then that within a year I would stop taking my gabapentin forever and learn to make peace with my new body, or that Erin's prediction would be spot-on and that my buzzy bottom never really would quiet down but that I would make my peace with that, too—that I would say to myself exactly what she had said to me: *so what?* That I would stand tall at my son's bar mitzvah—in flat shoes, yes, but beautiful flat shoes that would have made Dr. Zimcik proud. That I would finally, after months of fruitless searching, locate my second sit bone, which meant that sitting would become a far less precarious affair. That I would celebrate my fiftieth birthday with my closest friends and family and not once worry about falling over—and besides, there were enough people there to catch me if I did. That I would sometimes find myself thinking about that punky girl I met outside St. Mike's and marvel at her prescience because I *did* love Lyndhurst and how could I not? Because of Amanda and Dr. Zimcik and Rumy and my chorus of fascinating and caring nurses I had been, in so many ways, reborn. That my MRIs would continue to come back clean year after year. That all those stories I wrote from my bed, in my private room, in Unit 2B at the miraculous Lyndhurst spinal cord rehab clinic, would open the door to a new career, one that my father had wished I had chosen all those years ago—and that I had secretly wanted for myself for about as long as the tumor had been growing on my spine.

I looked at Rich. He was my dura, my protective covering. My love for him was boundless. I hoped he knew that I was his dura, too.

Acknowledgments

I am no one without my extraordinary family and friends.

My amazing mom and dad, who remained calm from the beginning, and who were (mostly) successful in hiding their fears from me. I have learned how to be a parent because of them and how to love because of them, the best teachers of all. To Rose Caplan, only the best mother-in-law. My beautiful sisters, Karen and Jackie, who were there for me always, making sure that not only was I taken care of but that my boys were, too. To Sheryl Brodey, Diane Flacks, Joanie Silverstein, and Elizabeth Marmur, my touchstones; Sheila Wilson, Laura Neinhuis, Judy Adelman Gershon, Michael Redhill, Paula Boudreau, Jeff Pustil, Kathy Laskey, Nadia Commodari, Miles Kronby, and Marc Lewin—for the lunches, the books, the visits, and the check-ins. Thank you all, my friends.

To Eleanor Domingo, for making sure that my kids were well-fed and well-played with.

Thank you to my mentor, Isabel Huggan, who I was so fortunate to be matched with through the Humber College Creative Writing Correspondence program. Her exhaustive help and inspiring insights helped me turn a fat, 500-plus page manuscript into something not only much slimmer, but also much better-looking.

Thank you to the hugely talented and gracious writer James Chatto, who, for a relatively small bribe (lunch, not even with wine), promised to read the first hundred pages of my book and, if they didn't suck, pass them on to his agent.

And thank you to that agent, the outstanding Bruce Westwood, at Westwood Creative Artists, and his equally outstanding, eagle-eyed assistant, Meg Wheeler. Together, you are an incredible dynamic duo. I am so grateful you took a flyer on me.

To my cousin Dr. Joel Finkelstein and my brilliant neurosurgeon, Dr. Howard Ginsberg. I cannot thank you both enough for what you did for me. Because of you, I can walk again.

And because of the patient, gentle, and superlative care of my physiotherapists at Lyndhurst, I can not only walk, but walk like a champ. I thank you every single day for this—especially Anne.

Thank you to Dr. Susan Brunt for tirelessly pursuing the source of my tingling feet. And to Dr. Heather Zimcik—because of your great listening skills, amazing outfits, and sense of humor, you ensured that my spirits did not flag.

Thank you to every last nurse I met along the way at St. Michael's Hospital and Toronto Rehab—Lyndhurst Centre. You are angels. Every day, you made me feel loved and cared for. I hope that, in even a small way, I was able to do the same for you. Especially Ramona, Paulina, and Olga.

Thank you to Kevin Hanson and the incredibly patient Sarah St. Pierre at Simon & Schuster. From our very first meeting, I thought: *Oh, I want to be here.* And thank you, too, to all the gems behind the scenes—Alison Woodbury, Ivy Mcfadden, Felicia Quon, Jessica Scott, Adria Iwasutiak, Lauren Morocco, Liz Whitehead, and Nancy Purcell—for their scrupulous work. And especially to my intuitive and brilliant editor, Nita Pronovost. Thank you for your enthusiasm and belief in me, and for pushing me to dig deeper and look more closely at the things that scared me most because you knew that's where all the good stuff lay.

And to my boys, Joey and Henry. You are both so damn smart and hilarious and also very, very good-looking. You were all the motivation I needed to get out of my chair and get my legs moving in the right direction, which was home to you.

And finally, to the love of my life, Rich Caplan. You are, quite simply, everything to me. Everything.

About the Author

© Maria Ricossa

RUTH MARSHALL, an actress for over twenty years, is probably best known for playing Clare's mom on *Degrassi: The Next Generation* and Billy Ray Cyrus's boss on *Doc*. She continues to do voice-over work for radio and television. Ruth lives with her family in Toronto, Ontario. *Walk It Off* is her first book.

@ruthmarshallwrites